ADRIANNE BLUE, an American who lives in London, was born in Washington DC, took an MA at Stanford University, California, and moved to Britain in 1977. She first made her reputation on *Time Out*, writing about sport and literature and acting as literary editor. She has contributed to a wide range of publications including the *Washington Post*, *Ms Magazine*, *Vogue*, *Cosmopolitan* and the *New Statesman*. A founding member of Britain's Women's Sport Foundation, she was also *City Limits'* first sports editor. She is currently working as a sports correspondent for *The Sunday Times*. Her first book, *Grace Under Pressure: The Emergence of Women in Sport*, was published to great acclaim in 1987.

FASTER, HIGHER, FURTHER

Women's Triumphs and Disasters at the Olympics

ADRIANNE BLUE

VIRAGO

For Madeleine

Published by VIRAGO PRESS Limited 1988
20−23 Mandela Street, London NW1 0HQ

Copyright © 1988 Adrianne Blue

British Library Cataloguing in Publication Data
Blue, Adrianne
Faster, higher, further: women in the olympics
1. Olympic games. Participation to 1988. Women
I. Title
796.4′8

ISBN 0-86068-648-5

Design by Jo Laws
Typeset by Rowland Phototypesetting Limited
Bury St Edmunds, Suffolk
Printed in Great Britain by
Mackays of Chatham Limited
Chatham, Kent

CONTENTS

STRETCHING THE LIMITS

OLYMPIC EYE: A SPORTWATCHER'S GUIDE

MOMENTOUS MOMENTS:
A CHRONOLOGY

1000 BC or earlier   The women-only Herean Games, probably the source of the Olympic idea, take place in Greece.

776 BC or earlier   Olympic rules forbid the men-only Games from taking place unless a priestess of Demeter is present.

440 BC   Kallipateira sneaks into the Olympics to see her son win, and the first Olympic sex test is devised to keep women out. Thereafter, coaches, like athletes, must register naked.

396 BC   The Spartan princess Kyniska becomes the first female Olympic champion when her horses win the chariot race.

1896   At the first modern Olympics, legend has it, a Greek woman called Melpomene (named for the Muse of Tragedy) runs an unofficial marathon in 4½ hours.

1900   Tennis player Charlotte Cooper of England, having won Wimbledon thrice, becomes the first female Olympic champion of the modern Games.

1908   Yachtswoman Frances Clytie Rivett-Carnac and her husband win gold, making her the first woman in any event to win against men. In a sister–brother Olympic double, archers Lottie Dod, one of the greatest sportswomen ever, and her brother William each win medals.

1912   The first Australian woman to win gold – and in world record time – Fanny Durack, puts the crawl on the world swimming map.

1928   Victorious Sonja Henie of Norway changes figure skating forever. But German runner Lina Radke's 800 metres triumph at the debut of women's track and field becomes a defeat for women when the distance is declared dangerous to the sex and removed from the Olympic calendar for thirty-six years.

1932   Texan 'Babe' Mildred Didrikson, the first successful female shamateur athlete, stars at the Los Angeles Olympics.

1948   At the first post-war Olympics in London, triumphant Fanny Blankers-Koen of the Netherlands becomes the first famous mother who runs.

1952   The first woman ever to compete in equestrian sport (against men), Lis Hartel, a Dane, wins a silver medal.

1956   The first woman in Olympic history to take the oath at the opening ceremony is skier Giuliana Chenal-Minuzzo, at the Winter Games in Italy.

1960   American sprinter Wilma Rudolph, who wore a leg brace as a child, wins three gold medals.

1964   The most successful sisters in Olympic history, Russians Irina and Tamara Press, are suspected of being men. Dawn Fraser becomes the only swimmer, male or female, to win the same event at three successive Olympics. Speed-skater Lydia Skoblikova wins her sixth gold medal, still a record total for either sex in any sport at the Winter Games.

1968   Enriqueta Basilio becomes the first woman to light an Olympic flame in the stadium. Peru, Poland and Mexico send women to compete in men's shooting events for the first time. But as the left hand giveth, the right hand taketh away: sex tests for women are introduced at these Mexican Games.

1972   Gymnast Olga Korbut launches a demure counter-revolution in Western sport. At 70, British equestrian Lorna Johnstone becomes the oldest-ever female Olympian.

1976   East German women show their might, winning eleven swimming and nine track and field golds of the possible fourteen in each sport. Pole Danuta Rosani is the first Olympic athlete disqualified for contravening drug regulations. American Margaret Murdock outshoots male riflemen to win silver.

1980   The greatest mother–daughter Olympic success occurs when Soviet runner Irina Nazarova, daughter of 1952 discus medalist Elizabeta Bagriantseva, wins gold in the relay.

1984   Joan Benoit wins the first women's Olympic marathon.

1988   Tennis returns to the Games, enshrining inequality with the agreement that fewer women than men be allowed to compete.

1992   Women's judo, a demonstration sport in 1988, becomes a fully fledged Olympic sport.

WOMEN AND MEN AT EACH OLYMPIAD

Summer

		Place	Date	Nations	Women	Men	Total
I	1896	Athens, Greece	6–15 April	13	–	311	311
II	1900	Paris, France	20 May–28 October	22	12	1318	1330
III	1904	St Louis, USA	1 July–23 November	13	8	617	625
*	1906	Athens, Greece	22 April–2 May	20	7	877	884
IV	1908	London, England	27 April–31 October	22	36	2020	2056
V	1912	Stockholm, Sweden	5 May–22 July	28	55	2491	2546
VI	1916	Berlin, Germany	Not held due to war	–	–	–	–
VII	1920	Antwerp, Belgium	20 April–12 September	29	64	2628	2692
VIII	1924	Paris, France	4 May–27 July	44	136	2956	3092
IX	1928	Amsterdam, Netherlands	17 May–12 August	46	290	2724	3014
X	1932	Los Angeles, USA	30 July–14 August	37	127	1281	1408
XI	1936	Berlin, Germany	1–16 August	49	328	3738	4066
XII	1940	Tokyo, then Helsinki	Not held due to war	–	–	–	–
XIII	1944	London, England	Not held due to war	–	–	–	–
XIV	1948	London, England	29 July–14 August	59	385	3714	4099
XV	1952	Helsinki, Finland	19 July–3 August	69	518	4407	4925
XVI	1956	Melbourne, Australia†	22 November–8 December	67	371	2813	3184
XVII	1960	Rome, Italy	25 August–11 September	83	610	4736	5346
XVIII	1964	Tokyo, Japan	10–24 October	93	683	4457	5140
XIX	1968	Mexico City, Mexico	12–27 October	112	781	4749	5530
XX	1972	Munich, FRG	26 August–10 September	122	1070	6086	7156
XXI	1976	Montreal, Canada	17 July–1 August	92	1251	4834	6085
XXII	1980	Moscow, Soviet Union	19 July–3 August	81	1088	4238	5326
XXIII	1984	Los Angeles, USA	28 July–12 August	140	1620	5458	7078
XXIV	1988	Seoul, South Korea	17 September–2 October	161	–	–	–
XXV	1992	Barcelona, Spain	–	–	–	–	–

Winter

		Place	Date	Nations	Women	Men	Total
I	1924	Chamonix, France	25 January–4 February	16	13	281	294
II	1928	St Moritz, Switzerland	11–19 February	25	27	468	495
III	1932	Lake Placid, USA	4–15 February	17	32	274	306
IV	1936	Garmisch-Partenkirchen, Germany	6–16 February	28	80	675	755
–	1940	Sapporo, then St Moritz, then Garmisch-Partenkirchen	Not held due to war	–	–	–	–
–	1944	Cortina d'Ampezzo, Italy	Not held due to war	–	–	–	–
V	1948	St Moritz, Switzerland	30 January–8 February	28	77	636	713
VI	1952	Oslo, Norway	14–25 February	30	109	623	732
VII	1956	Cortina d'Ampezzo, Italy	26 January–5 February	32	132	687	819
VIII	1960	Squaw Valley, USA	18–28 February	30	144	521	665
IX	1964	Innsbruck, Austria	29 January–9 February	36	200	986	1186
X	1968	Grenoble, France	6–18 February	37	212	1081	1293
XI	1972	Sapporo, Japan	3–13 February	35	217	1015	1232
XII	1976	Innsbruck, Austria	4–15 February	37	228	900	1128
XIII	1980	Lake Placid, USA	13–24 February	37	234	833	1067
XIV	1984	Sarajevo, Yugoslavia	8–19 February	49	276	1002	1278
XV	1988	Calgary, Canada	13–28 February	57	317	1128	1445
XVI	1992	Albertville, France	–	–	–	–	–

* Tenth anniversary Games, official but not numbered.
† This total includes the 13 women and 146 men who took part in the equestrian events, which were held in Stockholm.

STRETCHING THE LIMITS

CHAPTER 1

ELBOWING IN: AN OVERVIEW

No one wanted women at the Olympics. We cajoled, we argued the case logically, and then, little by little, event by event, we elbowed our way in. The triumphs and disasters that followed would never have happened if we had waited to be asked. Manners have their uses, but they often mean things take a long time. Few people had better manners than the Baron Pierre de Coubertin, whose dream of a modern Olympics – which did not include women – became reality in 1896. It was Coubertin's genteel belief that 'Women have but one task, that of crowning the winner with garlands'. He cited as precedent the Olympics of ancient Greece where, it was said, only men took part. This is not quite so.

Very early on, when the ancient Games were a religious festival, Olympic rules required a priestess of the goddess Demeter to be present as a witness, or the Games could not take place. This priestess was always a married woman, and is said by some sources to have been the lone woman at the Games. But can you imagine a respectable, religious matron agreeing to go as the solitary female to a festival where men went naked? Or even where, as in the very earliest days, they strutted about in shorts? Just how many women attended is unknown. The ancient sources, all written centuries after the event, are inconsistent. The historian Pausanias says that any woman found at the Olympics would be thrown off the cliffs of the nearby mountain. But he also says that virgins were not refused admission. Other reports speak of prostitutes being welcomed at

Unheralded victory: Steffi Graf's at the Olympic tennis demonstration, Los Angeles, 1984

'Women have but one task, that of crowning the winner with garlands'

Baron Pierre de Coubertin, 1902

the Games. And there were, of course, women who sneaked in. One of them, Kallipateira, was the daughter or the widow of a great sportsman, either a runner or a boxer. Her son, who had trained hard in the family sport, was to compete at the Games in 440 BC. Kallipateira encouraged him, and may even have been one of those who coached him. She was damned if she wasn't going to be there to see him win. So she put on a loose, shapeless robe – only the athletes had to be naked – and watched the action in the section reserved for coaches and managers. There were many inconveniences: flies, dust, rowdy crowds of sweaty spectators. No doubt she paid little attention to the naked young men: like any coach, she had proud eyes only for her athlete. And when he won, she rushed over the fence to hug him. That is when she was spotted as a female.

The story goes that because Kallipateira had been born into or married into a good sporting family – that is, because she was allied to power – no terrible punishment befell her. Remember, too, she had coached a winner. There is nothing the masculine world admires more than a winner and it therefore puts up with his or her entourage. But to make sure there were no more Kallipateiras at the Games, the ancient gentlemen devised the first Olympic sex test: thereafter, coaches as well as athletes had to parade and register in the nude.

Despite the macho aura of sport, the concept, the very idea of the ancient Olympics, had been 'borrowed' from the women-only Herean Games, which had been going on at least since 1000 BC, and probably much, much longer. (The first firm record of the Olympics is 776 BC, but they too probably started a few centuries earlier.) The Herean Games were held at Olympia every four years and consisted of a foot race, which women ran in age groups. The Olympics too took place at four-year intervals, initially had just one foot race, and were, like the *Heraia*, held for religious purposes. Every winner at the Herean and Olympic Games got the same prize – a victory crown of olive branches, a portion of the cow which was sacrificed at the festival, and the right to leave a miniature statue of herself or himself at the Temple.

The Olympic Games lasted in Greece for about fifteen hundred years. The Herean Games continued for much – possibly all – of this time. Because of religious conservatism, the elders of Olympia never allowed more than the foot race at the women's games, and maintained the separation, the sexual apartheid. This was not a typical policy of the ancient Greeks. At Sparta, on the theory that strong mothers gave birth to tough soldiers, girls had always undertaken the same athletic exercise as boys. Plato advocated running and fencing for women. And by the Christian era most of the major Greek games did have women's events.[1]

No one knows for sure when the last Olympics took place. The date usually given is AD 393, the year a decree by the first Christian Emperor of Rome, Theodosius I, banned pagan cults. But the Olympics may have dragged on another thirty-four years or so, until the Temple of Zeus at Olympia was burned to the ground after Theodosius II ordered all pagan temples to be destroyed.[2]

By then the Olympic Games had long since become a corrupt parody of what they had been. In their heyday from the sixth century AD to the second century BC, they were a lot like what they are now. But worse. Some of the events were bloody, some deadly. Athletes were professionals instead of muscular amateurs. Glory and religious observance as motivations had been replaced by gold.

But eight hundred years before the demise of the ancient Olympics, history records that a Spartan princess called Kyniska became the first female Olympic champion, when her horses won the chariot race in 396 BC. The ancient historian Plutarch, puzzled as to why a woman should want to enter, came up with the answer that it was her brother's idea. If her costly chariot, her paid charioteer and expensive horses won, the brother is said to have argued, it would show that drachmas, not daring and skill, were what counted. In other words, the prince wanted his sister the princess to protest the unfairness, the privileged position that the royal and rich had at the Games. Not likely.

The issue of money, the fact that governments or athletes can buy Olympic medals by spending huge amounts on equipment, training and the like, is still much argued. But it wasn't what motivated Kyniska:

> Sparta's kings were fathers and brothers of mine,
> But since with my chariot and storming horses, I, Kyniska
> Have won the prize, I place my portrait here
> And proudly proclaim
> That of all Grecian women I first bore the crown.[3]

As this record of her Olympic victory suggests, Kyniska had a very simple reason for entering: she wanted to win.

In Paris, in 1900, at the second modern Olympics, Charlotte 'Chattie' Cooper, who lived within easy bicycling distance of Wimbledon and had won the singles championship there three times, became the first female Olympic champion of the modern Games. Her 6–1, 6–4 victory over Hélène Prévost was popular only on the English side of the Channel. Cooper won the mixed doubles too.

She had a lovely attacking game, unusual for the time, and was, according to Commander George Hillyard, her contemporary, 'a quite unusually strong and active girl, with a constitution like the proverbial ostrich, who scarcely knew what it was to be tired, and was never sick or sorry. She once told me she had heard of such things but did not know what a headache was.'

Tennis had squeezed into the modern Olympics – there were 1,318 men and twelve women at the Paris Games – largely because it was a game played by women of a certain social standing. Modest, well-bred, well-educated – 'ladies' – the tennis players were thought to be, and were. They were also – and some of them knew it – heralding a revolution in women's sport.

The glitzy stars of the 1920s played at the Olympics. The French tennis diva Suzanne Lenglen, who often drank cognac between sets, won in 1920. The American doctor's dour daughter Helen Wills (later Moody), known as Miss Poker Face, won in 1924. Then, unable to agree with the Olympic fathers about money or power, tennis stormed out of the Olympics.

The tennis types were rather modern amateurs, used to receiving expensive 'courtesies'. They stayed at posh hotels where no bill was presented and received as gifts Parisian designer clothes. Lenglen's were by Patou. The gentlemen of the International Olympic Committee (IOC) had a far more puritanical definition of what constituted an amateur. Athletes, they felt, whatever the sport, should be born rich or stay poor.

Moreover, the IOC wanted major tennis events like the Wimbledon championships to be cancelled during an Olympic year so as not to steal the thunder of the Games. This, to the gentlemen of the International Lawn Tennis Federation, was unthinkable.

Tennis, the oldest Olympic sport for women, is also the newest, reappearing at the 1988 Olympics. In 1900, the players zealously guarded their amateur standing. In 1988, Steffi Graf, Hana Mandlikova and other top professional tennis players – women whose earnings from sport are in the millions, whether you count in pounds or dollars or even in Deutschmarks – have been nominated

Charlotte Cooper, the first female Olympic champion of the modern Games

'Steffi is an incredible talent'

Billie Jean King

'It's easy. It's all timing'

Steffi Graf

by their national tennis associations. Graf, the West German prodigy, who started playing at the age of four and who, in 1988 at the age of eighteen, was ranked number one in the world, won the demonstration tennis event at the 1984 Los Angeles Olympics. The famous did not play at Los Angeles. Young Graf was then still a talented, accident-prone unknown. But Seoul 1988 is another ball game.

To be eligible, players nominated by their countries must stop earning prize money for just *two weeks* before the Games. This very modern definition of amateur is not inconsistent with the way things are going generally at the Olympics. Tennis players may be the richest Olympians, but track and field stars and swimmers, skiers and figure skaters, are doing very nicely too (see also Chapter 12, Arguing Points).

What victory meant to Chattie Cooper is not far different from what it means to Steffi Graf. But there is an entirely new slant to the issue of money. Philippe Chatrier, the president of the International Tennis Federation, argues that one reason for his sport rejoining the Olympics is to get more money for tennis players who are not stars. 'There is a limited amount of public funds available in Africa, South America and Asia, and priority is always given to Olympic sports,' he says. 'This was one of the reasons we fought so hard to return tennis to the Olympics.' There are 124 nations in the ITF. 'Some Olympic officials insist the Olympics should be reserved for amateurs,' Chatrier concludes. 'This is like a very bad joke.'[4]

It is no bad thing that the argument that the Olympics should be for unpaid amateurs, so bitterly fought for three-quarters of a century, has decidedly been lost. It was a wrong-headed idea that would have limited the sport to those with private incomes or friends with private incomes. What is worrying is that the return of tennis to the Games has furthered inequality, with fewer women than men in the Olympic draw. At Seoul, the plan is that sixty-four men and forty-eight women will play.

The unladylike sport of track and field athletics had trouble getting into the Games. It was reluctantly admitted, as part of a deal to get rid of the female lobbyists, in 1928. Women were already competing at archery, golf (discontinued), swimming, yachting, figure skating and fencing. The centrepiece of the Olympics has always been track and field events. But the gentlemen in charge resisted any such events for women largely because to perform them properly women had to breathe heavily, look messy and sweat; they might also have to develop a little muscle; all of which seemed to the Olympic fathers to be the sort of atrocity which would bring civilization down. They were in fact correct on one point. Civilization as they knew it was changing: women were about to get a fairer shake. But not, of course, without a few more slaps in the face.

The deal was this. The women had been staging their own international athletics games since 1921, when a hundred women competed in Monte Carlo in the javelin, high jump, shotput, and six running events, the longest being the 800 metres. Three hundred women competed in Monte Carlo the following year. The goal of the international women's sporting union, the Fédération Sportive Feminine Internationale (FSFI), which put on this event, was to get women athletes into the Olympics. Now they put on their own mini-Olympics, first in France, then in Sweden, the latter with thirteen events. They wanted to call their games the Women's Olympics, but gave the idea up because it greatly dismayed the

Only men competed, but in London in 1908 these Danish gymnasts gave quite a demonstration

men's athletics union. The women of the FSFI combined pushiness with placatory behaviour – and, at last, the men's union, the International Amateur Athletics Federation (IAAF) consented to take over and ratify women's records, and see that they got into the Olympics – albeit with only five events.

At the 1928 Amsterdam Olympics all began well. Anni Holdman of Germany won the first heat of the 100 metres and became the winner of the first women's athletics event. The next day, the discus thrower Halina Konopacka of Poland won the first athletics gold medal.

Then, amid much misgiving, came the 800 metres. Many thought the distance too long for the weaker sex, but the women had insisted that the 800 metres race be part of the deal. Few had had much opportunity to run the supposedly dangerous distance, but many wanted to, even though they understood that the lengthy 800 metres was an exhausting race for women. Talk about psychological barriers: by the time this race was held, for most of the women in it, the barrier was a mental mountain.

Lina Radke climbed it, relying on her solid stride to carry her to victory in 2 minutes 16.8 seconds. Less than a second behind Radke of Germany came Kinuye Hitomi of Japan, and a mere 0.2 seconds behind her was Inga Gentzel of Sweden. The first six finished within ten seconds of each other, the first three bettering the world record. Some runners collapsed either before or after the finish. This is not uncommon in hotly contested races; but nevertheless the distance was declared dangerous to women and removed from the Olympic calendar. Radke's 800-metres triumph at the debut of women's track and field had become a defeat for women.

Twenty-five years later, one of the men who witnessed the race, the former Olympian Harold Abrahams, whose own victory is chronicled in the film *Chariots of Fire*, urged its reinstatement: 'The 800 metres was a scene of a very limited amount of distress among the defeated competitors, and somewhat sensational writing by many of the journalists present resulted in that event being omitted. It should and may be included again at Rome in 1960.'[5]

It was. But damage had been done during the thirty-six years that women were 'protected' from running 800 metres or longer at the Olympics. The development of women's track had been markedly slowed down, though it could not be completely stifled. The 1,500 metres – four minutes on the track – was the longest Olympic distance for women until 1984, when the 3,000 metres (less than

8.35 minutes) and the marathon (2 hours 24.52 minutes) were added. Men had been running long distances since the start of the modern Games.

The first female athlete to become an Olympic star was the muscley all-rounder from Texas, 'Babe-Don't-Call-Me-Mildred' Didrikson, who was the sensation of the 1932 Los Angeles Games. Since then, there have been many stars, some of whose stories are told in this book. Amid rationing and rain, in London in 1948, the Dutch runner Fanny Blankers-Koen showed how much could be accomplished by a 'blonde mother of two' who was supposedly past it. Dawn Fraser, the swimmer who always got in trouble unless she was in the pool, made her Olympic debut in 1956.

Olga Korbut, the childlike Russian gymnast who brought her sport to the attention of millions in 1972, proved that troublemakers need not be brash or overtly muscular. The tiny Romanian Nadia Comaneci and the even tinier American Mary Lou Retton made their contributions to Killer Gymnastics too.

Wilma Rudolph's is an almost unbelievable tale of triumph against the odds. She grew up in a huge, poor, black family in the American South, one of the youngest of about twenty brothers and sisters. 'I had to be fast, otherwise there was nothing left to eat on the table,' she once quipped. Her father was a Tennessee sharecropper: as well as poverty, the family faced severe racial prejudice.

Illnesses – double pneumonia, scarlet fever and polio – racked Wilma Rudolph's childhood. When she was six, her right leg became paralysed from the polio. The members of the family took turns massaging it four times a day. When she was eight, she could walk with a leg brace. When she was nearly twelve, she traded the brace for corrective shoes. She played basketball with her brothers, and when the shoes began to seem unwieldy, she played barefoot. She was good enough to make the high-school team.

Then she had a try at running. By the age of fifteen she was winning state-wide competitions, at sixteen she made her Olympic debut, at twenty in Rome, at the 1960 Olympics, she won triple gold, including the prestigious 100-metres title – this from a woman who couldn't walk unaided until she was approaching her teens. Not surprisingly, she was the talk of the Games. Wilma Rudolph was the first of what would be a long line of great black American sprinters.

Wyomia Tyus, who belonged to the same running club as Rudolph, the Tennessee Tigerbells, won the 100 metres at the next

'My goal was to be the greatest athlete that ever lived'
Babe Didrikson

9

'They talk about an "open" Olympics. No amount of money could pay me for the thrill I got'

Wilma Rudolph, 1960
Olympic champion

two Games. Tennessee State University, which both sprinters attended, has been a home to women runners for three decades. The third black American to win the 100 metres was Evelyn Ashford, at the 1984 Olympics. She grew up in an army family, largely in California. At her high school in 1970 there was no running team for girls, so she ran with the boys.

At the other end of the running scale is the gruelling 26-mile 385-yard marathon. Although a Greek woman named Melpomene is said to have run an unsanctioned marathon at the very first modern Games, women did not get an official chance at the distance until Los Angeles 1984.

The greatest collision since the Titanic and the iceberg, quoth *The Times*, was that of Zola Budd and Mary Decker Slaney in Los Angeles in 1984. Their collision on the track in the 3,000 metres final was as much about politics as sport. And no matter what anyone pretends, sport and politics are old friends. At the Hitler Games, as the 1936 Berlin Olympics were known, that friendship succeeded in putting undue pressure on the Jewish fencer Hélène Mayer (see Chapter 2).

There are very few events in which women compete against men. In these open events, women have done well. In 1908, Frances Rivett-Carnac with her husband won the yachting gold medal in the 7 metres class. She became the first woman to win in an event in any sport which was not restricted to women or to mixed pairs. In 1952, Lis Hartel, a Dane, the first woman ever to compete in Olympic equestrian sport, won a silver medal. In 1968 Peru, Poland and Mexico sent women to compete in men's shooting events for the first time. The first woman to compete came thirteenth in the skeet event – not bad. The first to win a medal was the American Margaret Murdoch, who outshot riflemen to win silver in 1976. (See Chapter 11, Arguing Points, for a full discussion of the red-herring issue of women vs. men in sport.)

At Mexico in 1968, a woman carried the Olympic torch into the stadium for the first time and lit the flame. But it was at these Mexican Games that sex tests for women were introduced. The most successful sisters in Olympic history, Russians Irina and Tamara Press, retired amid suspicion of being men. Perhaps they were, but there were a handful of other reasons they might have retired (see pp. 160–1).

Princess Anne at the 1976 Olympics fell off her horse, but remounted and rode on, despite being badly injured. What was that nonsense they used to teach us in fairy tales about the princess and the pea? My childhood's version spoke of a princess who was so delicate, so hoity-toity, that when a tiny pea was lodged under her thick mattress she found it so annoying she could not sleep. None of the top riders today are coal miners' daughters; they tend to come from comfortable backgrounds, as horses and feed, and trainers and stables, are costly. But these equestrians are a tough and courageous lot – the American Karen Stives and the Briton Virginia Holgate Leng are but two who have returned from very serious injury.

Judo is another sport that requires bravery as well as skill. Partly because it costs little to practise, it has in recent years attracted girls and women from working-class families worldwide. It is widely contested, and it is deplorable that women's judo has had such a tardy acceptance at the Games: a demonstration sport in 1988, not a fully fledged Olympic sport until 1992.

The *Wunderfrauen*, the East German Wonder Women, are a force to be reckoned with on the track and in the pool. They have been derided as monsters of sports science, the ugly products of the East German sports machine, but are they?

The most famous legend in East German sport, Marita Koch, who was born in 1957 and retired honourably in 1986, topped the world in two events, the 200 and 400 metres, over a twelve-year span. She, like most of the others, does not conform to the Huge Monster Woman stereotype: she was of only middling size for an athlete, five foot seven inches tall (171 cm), weighing in at 143 pounds. The hallmark of her career was consistency. She had more than a fair share of injuries, but rarely had an off-day. Koch reset the world 400-metres record seven times (her fastest being 47.60 seconds), and the 200-metres four times (fastest, 21.71 seconds). In all she set sixteen outdoor world records. Injury blighted her 1976 Olympic hopes, but in 1980, she became the Olympic 400-metres champion, and picked up a silver medal at 100 metres. Then she concentrated on 200 metres and might well have won the Olympic title in Los Angeles in 1984, had the Eastern bloc not boycotted the Games. At the end of her running career, Koch married Wolfgang Meier, who had coached her from the beginning.

The leaner, lankier, taller Heike Drechsler, who is five foot eleven, has bettered Koch's world 200-metres record. Seven years younger than Koch, she too has had a steady rise, both as a sprinter and as a long jumper. In the latter event, in 1981 she was European junior champion, becoming in 1983, at eighteen, the youngest world champion; in 1986, she became European champion and set a new world record. That year – her first as a sprinter – she became European 200-metres champion and equalled the world record. Then she reset it.

Drechsler has been married since 1984 to Andreas Drechsler, a football goalkeeper whom she has known since she was fourteen. She has known her coach since she was twelve.

In 1987, in the heat of a Roman September, another East German began to attract worldwide attention. The newcomer, 123-pound Silke Gladisch, who was five foot four – a head shorter than Drechsler, and also smaller than Koch – now won the world 200-metres championship. The East German sports 'machine' had found women of tremendously varying size and shape to lead the world. Ironically, Gladisch might have done better had she been born in another country: 'We had such good sprinters, it was very difficult for me to break into the top rank.'

Gladisch, who was born in 1964, had trained for years with Marita Koch, who belonged to the same running club. 'For many years in Rostock, I was training with Marita, but I didn't feel at the time that I was in her shadow. It was good experience as we always trained side by side.' Gladisch says she felt Koch's decision to retire as a blow: 'It was a very hard time for me. For a while it was hard to find the motivation to go it alone.'

Now Silke Gladisch (who since the 1987 world championship has married Dieter Moeller and may change her name in the record books) has high Olympic hopes.

The other half of the Koch-Gohr legend of the past decade is Marlies Gohr, the first woman to crack eleven seconds for the 100 metres. Marlies Gohr is five foot five, exactly the same height as the American runner Evelyn Ashford and of about the same medium build. Known for her light, pattering step, Gohr took on the 100-metres sprint mantle from another East German, the 1972 Olympic champion Renate Stecher, a massive big-boned, heavy-footed woman.

For ten years, Marlies Gohr and Evelyn Ashford battled the distance to see who was the fastest woman in the world. Gohr set three new world records; then Ashford set two. Ashford became the 1984 Olympic champion; East Germany wasn't there.

Re-enter petite Silke Gladisch, who won not only the 200-metres world championship in Rome, but also the 100 metres. Gladisch

Next stop Seoul: Heike Drechsler (*right*) congratulating double world champion Silke Gladisch in Rome, 1987

**'The secret of
swimming
success? If I
knew, I
wouldn't tell
you'**

Anke Mohring, European
champion 1987

hadn't believed she could win both titles, but her coach, Wolfgang
Meier, told her it was possible.

Koch, Gohr, Drechsler, Gladisch – winners, one after another. But
what kind of sports machine 'manufactures' products of such
diversity? It is evidently a careful, intelligent one. PE and sports
club teachers in East Germany are always on the look out for the
athletically gifted child – as indeed they are in the West. The
difference is that the child is given the chance to go to a school that
specializes in her sport. The school is said to be voluntary, and most
likely is. East or West it is the rare parent or child who, when told
the future holds sports stardom, would decline.

Sports clubs are very important. Heike Drechsler belongs to the
famous Motor Jena Sports Club, whose most famous member used
to be Marlies Gohr. Twenty per cent of the population is said to
belong to the national sports union, many of them children under
six, who pay something monthly – a tiny amount – for the privilege.
All children aged from seven to ten are taught to swim. No wonder
there are so many fine swimmers; there is an enormous reservoir of
talent to choose from – the entire population.

The achievement of the Eastern Europeans has spurred Western
nations to give a little more time and money to their women. All of
the East Europeans, it has been charged, are full-time professionals,
supported by the state. In reality, however, there are very few
Western athletes who stand an Olympic chance who are not also
training full-time. Depending on which country they live in, they
may get scholarships, grants, unemployment compensation, and, if
they can, sponsorship and endorsement money.

In the West, however, the system doesn't recognize a responsibility to see to it that an athlete gets the education or training she
needs so that she has a *modus vivendi* after she winds up her career.

But is the East German system monstrous and inhumane? Do
they pump their athletes full of anabolic steroids and growth
hormone? It is very likely that these or other drugs have been and
are used in East Germany, as they are elsewhere. But the heptathlete Birgit Dressel, who died in agony in 1987 after regularly taking a
huge medley of drugs, including banned ones, – many (if not all)
prescribed by her country's most respected sports doctor – was a
West German. After her death, Birgit Dressel's coach 'recalled' that
the anabolic agent Megagrisevit, which she took every day, had
come anonymously through the post.[6]

Many – perhaps most – of the world's star sportsmen and

sportswomen use drugs in some sort of cycle. The cycle enables them to be 'clean' when it comes time for a drugs test. Fewer women than men use the drugs, largely because of the traditional fear of muscle in females.

Anabolic steroids are synthetic versions of the male hormone testosterone and enable an athlete of either sex to build muscle quickly. The drugs are not magic: they may enable an athlete to do three training sessions a day instead of two. But without hard training along enlightened lines, the most noticeable effect the drugs will have is not strength, but acne. (See Chapter 11, Arguing Points, for further discussion of drug abuse).

The first East German women's Olympic team picked up a handful of medals at the 1968 and 1972 Games (until then, even after the war, the Germanies had entered one team). In 1976 the East Germans won eleven swimming and nine track and field golds of the possible fourteen in each of the sports. That is when the rumours about East Germany got nasty; less emphasis was given to the fact that the Australians and the Americans and others had also been using sport science for years.

There is no proof that the East Germans are worse drug offenders than anyone else, though there have been allegations of athletes being forced to take drugs. But most athletes who take illegal muscle-building drugs don't have to be forced. And as I have said, many athletes in many sports, in most countries, have been using drugs for years. They may not have been using them as wisely as the East Germans. What the East Germans did do was learn as much as they could about training as soon as they could, and they made the country's considerable sporting facilities as available, or nearly as available, to women as to men. Their motivation, however, was less equal rights than more medals.

Today, despite the lingering ambivalence toward sportswomen, despite the bigotry, Olympic champions are women to be reckoned with. They are there, on the track, in the pool, on the court, in the arena. Female Olympians are far more numerous now, and far more accomplished, than they were in 1900; but they still find themselves, without wanting to be, on the frontier of conventional notions of femininity.

It takes toughness to win in any sport. It takes perseverance to win, hard training, concentration, muscles. To some people, big biceps are ugly. To some people, they are threatening. To Olym-

pians they are necessary tools of the trade. But strong bodies are only the half of it; strong minds are as necessary. Sport helps women blossom to full womanhood.

It is sometimes said that most serious sportswomen and certainly the female Olympians have followed the male model of sport. That is to say, they play to win. They have mastered (oh what a male-sounding word) the skills of the game, they have mastered themselves; they have striven hard. Is this truly manly, or is it human? In sport, someone always wins, someone loses; one's accomplishment is judged and rated. Achievement may be golden, silver, or lowly bronze. One competes, competes, competes. Some women, among them some feminists, have been put off sport because of these factors. Some see in sports little more than an exercise of power.

But the secret of attaining greatness in sport is attempting to compete against oneself – that is, trying to get better at one's work, one's art. Most Olympic champions yearn to be the best they can be and hope that that is the best in the world. One of the brawny, brilliant discus throwers of the 1950s, Olga Fikotova, a Czech who married an American hammer thrower and became Olga Connolly, puts it this way: 'Humans have been equipped with a wondrous range of creative movement. Motion is a basic element of life, and sports are the milieu wherein a human being can express her physical genius.' A champion extends the sense of possibility for us all. Sport may or may not be the people's art. It may or may not be a hard-nosed profession. But to engage in sport even more than to watch it is a source of pleasure – no, of joy.

This book celebrates and assesses the achievements of the century's great Olympians, exploring their motivations and recapturing the moments which have forced them into the sporting memory. Not all of the Olympic story is happy; not all of it is admirable. The story of one Korean woman whose Olympic hopes were stifled years ago comes to mind as we look forward to the 1988 Games, set to take place in strife-ridden Seoul, Korea, despite years of riots in the street, tear gas, shooting, death; despite the ill-tempered truce between North and South Korea.

Only once before have the summer Olympics taken place in Asia; that was in Tokyo, in 1964, where the games, held amid modern splendour, were overall a gargantuan success. But for Sin Kim Dan from North Korea, one of the finest runners of her generation, the Games were a disappointment. She was the fastest woman in the world at 400 and 800 metres. Her 51.9-second 400-metres record,

World judo champion Karen Briggs throws European champion Diane Bell in practice

17

set in 1962, was not bettered until 1969; her unsanctioned 1963 and 1964 800-metres records, the fastest being 1 minute 58.0 seconds, were not bettered until 1973. Sin Kim Dan had been expected to win both medals in Tokyo, but she never got to compete.

Along with all other athletes who had taken part the year before in the Games of the New Emerging Forces in Indonesia, known as the GANEFO Games, she was barred from the Olympics. The new GANEFO Games, a celebration of Third-World muscle staged by President Sukarno in Djakarta, in which Sin Kim Dan had competed as a member of the North Korean team, were deemed politically motivated (as indeed they were). The Olympics, however, where teams also compete country by country for national prestige, were not seen as political.

For Sin Kim Dan the trip to Tokyo was sad, but not entirely wasted. She had a five-minute reunion with her father whom she had not seen since the start of the Korean War fourteen years before.

The story of women's triumphs and (less frequently) disasters at the Olympics is full of incident. There are many, almost too many, extraordinary tales to tell. The moments highlighted in this book have been chosen not just for drama but because they are, as well, significant occasions. These great sporting moments were important to these women and to all women. The Olympic motto is 'Faster, Higher, Stronger'. Women are going faster, higher, and further than ever before at the Olympics. And to do this they have to be stronger. But we haven't seen the half of it yet.

CHAPTER 2

DALLAS CYCLONE

*T*he high-school girls getting out of their basketball bloomers
and into their sweaters and skirts were startled when the
Colonel, with his rain-darkened gray Stetson in his hand and his
plaid overcoat slung over his arm, barged into the locker room
immediately after the game. But no one mistook him for a 'masher'.
On that cold, rainy Texas night in 1930, the Colonel, who was
ex-army, looked exactly like what he was – an insurance-company
basketball scout.

He had come two hundred miles from Dallas to scout a forward
on the Houston team, but it was Mildred Didrikson who impressed
him. Quick, wiry, *tough*, Didrikson, who played for the hick-town
high-school team, the Miss Royal Purples, seemed unable to miss a
basket. She had exquisite timing. And skill.

In the locker room, the Colonel offered sixteen-year-old[1] Mildred
Didrikson a job – $1,080 a year, or $90 a month – to become a
stenographer at Employers Casualty of Dallas and play 'amateur'
basketball for the company team, the Golden Cyclones. It was a
fortune at the time: a farmhand got $220, a steelworker $423, a
typist $624, and the Depression was on. Mildred Didrikson, who
came from a large, poor, Norwegian immigrant family, threw a
spitball out the window and told the Colonel she would let him
know.

Neither Mildred Didrikson nor the Colonel had any idea that her
decision would be an historic moment in Olympic sport. Brash,
flamboyant, 'Don't-Call-Me-Mildred' Babe Didrikson, 'girl red-
neck', who spat and bragged and showed off her rippling biceps,
who made no concessions to femininity, would become more
famous and more admired than any demure Miss America. Head-

**Publicity shot
for the 1932
Olympics**

Above: Helen Madison winning the glamour event of the pool, 100 metres, Los Angeles, 1932.
Left: Babe Didrikson winning the javelin

'She was lanky and boyish-looking with very short hair'

Hurdler Evelyne Hall

lines, ticker-tape parades, track and field world records and golf dates with the President were to be her future. This female Olympic 'shamateur' would make a worldwide reputation by winning and winning and winning on a single magical summer afternoon at the 1932 Olympic trials. A few weeks later, at the Los Angeles Games, she would do it again.

A supreme all-rounder, Babe Didrikson excelled at a dozen sports. From 1930 to 1932 she held American, Olympic or world records in five different track and field events, and was ranked high enough as a basketball player to be given the honorary title All-American. Her batting average in a Dallas softball league was 400, and she could punt a football 75 yards. She could swim close to world-record time in the sprints, although swimming was never a sport she took seriously. She became the first American to win the British Ladies' Amateur golf championship. In all, she won eighty-two golf tournaments. One year she won seventeen in a row.

Nearly a quarter of a century after her still-unequalled Olympic achievement, a poll of the American public named Babe Didrikson as the greatest woman athlete of the first half of the twentieth century.

By then, too, she had long since landed women's sport with what some saw as an uncomfortably butch image. Gertrude Ederle's record-breaking English Channel swim in 1926, and Amelia Earhart's solo transatlantic flight in May 1932, had also led to exuberant headlines and parades. Independent, athletic women were somewhat in vogue. Babe, with her cropped hair and her disdain for sissies, was the darling of sportswriters. But even then, mothers began to warn their daughters off baseball and into ballet or even tap-dancing. In Babe Didrikson's hometown of Beaumont, Texas, one sports-mad girl remembers her mother saying, 'Just don't be like the Babe, that's all I ask.' It is not at all likely that a victorious Mildred Didrikson coming to prominence in the reactionary 1950s would have become so well-loved an American sweetheart. But let's not get ahead of the story.

Home, in Beaumont, Texas, Mildred Didrikson put the case bluntly: 'I've got to make something of my athletic ability now or never – I'm not gonna be good always, you know.' She asked Papa and Mama for permission to drop out of school and move to Dallas. Beaumont – no paradise – was a small refinery town which stank of oil. Air pollution was not an issue yet, but in Beaumont the smog was already there. The nine Didriksons lived at 850 Doucette

Avenue, in the down-at-the-heels south end of town. The Magnolia Refinery was at one end of the street; the railroad tracks were at the other.

Babe's father was Ole Didriksen – Babe changed the spelling from *sen* to *son*. Possibly she thought it sounded more American. Her father had been a ship's carpenter. Now he did rough carpentry and, when he could get it, cabinet work for better-off Texans. He had settled first in Port Arthur, no oasis either. On her arrival from clear-skied Norway, his wife wept.

Mildred, the sixth child and youngest girl, gifted at every sport she tried, was on every girls' team at school. Her best academic subject was typing: she won a typing contest – a keyboard race.

Behind the house on Doucette Avenue, her father had built an outdoor gymnasium. All seven children used it. There was even a trapeze. Babe Didrikson's sister Lillie played there with Babe, who was two years younger but far more skilful. 'We pretended we was in the circus, hangin' by our feet, tryin' to hang by our teeth even, Babe was the best, even better than the boys.'[2] When Babe was about twelve, she and Lillie visited a family friend who worked in a circus in California. There Babe learned to walk a tightrope. At many sports, she outplayed the boys. In high school, the football coach thought she was so good that he wanted her on his team, but he was overruled.

Baseball was her favourite sport. 'She hit so many home runs, that girl did, that someone said she was just like Babe Ruth [the baseball idol of the day] and so that's how she got that name,' Lillie says. Maybe it is true that someone else first called Mildred Didrikson 'Babe'. Later, though, she insisted on the name herself.

Now, before she could move to Dallas, she had to have permission from her parents. Babe's sister remembers the family discussion in which Babe and Papa did most of the talking. Papa Didriksen is said to have chewed on his pipe and considered the best course for his tomboy daughter. She had no boyfriend; no domestic bent; no better prospect. Girls' basketball – played by school and company teams – was the most popular women's team sport in the country. Well-bred young ladies drew modest audiences at the expensive Eastern seaboard women's colleges. Farmgirls and millworkers' daughters in the Middle West played to large, raucous crowds.

Mama, who had skated and skied in Norway, but who had in America become a highly traditional hausfrau, had made it clear

'I came out here to beat everybody in sight'

Babe Didrikson

that she didn't like the idea of her youngest girl alone in Dallas.

Papa suddenly said in Norwegian-accented English: 'Goddom-mit, yes. She will go.'

Mama went into the kitchen. A while later, Babe's sister Lillie followed her and saw that Mama's eyes were red and swollen from crying.

Babe withdrew from high school on 14 February 1930. The Miss Royal Purples's loss was to be the Dallas Cyclones's gain. She was one of the best investments Employers Casualty would ever make. When the Golden Cyclones played, they won, and the company got column inches in the papers. It was free advertising. Soon it was national. Her first season, the team finished runners-up in the national championship. Babe, the star, was ranked high enough nationally to win an All-American listing. That year, Colonel McCombs, who was also the coach, entered the Cyclones in the national track and field championships too. They wore bright yellow suits emblazoned with the words 'Employers Casualty Insurance'.

Evelyne Hall, a hurdler from Chicago, met Babe at those 1930 national championships. 'She was sprawled on the ground and her teammates were around her. They were very proud and they kept saying what a great ballplayer she was. I liked her, too. At this time, she was a modest, likeable girl. She was lanky and boyish-looking with very short hair, but that was the style then.'

The following year, Hall didn't like Babe so much. Babe now entered the hurdles event, and Hall lost to her in the heats. More-over she seemed to Hall to have every advantage. 'Our team', said Hall, 'didn't have any money. We were poor. We each had a pair of track shoes, but the points were worn down to nothing.' Babe had had the longest, sharpest spikes on the track, and, according to Hall, she had the biggest ego. 'At this point, Babe was pretty cocky. Everyone was doing things for her. If she wanted a drink of water, someone got it for her. She seemed to have managers; her team-mates waited on her. She didn't snub me, but she was not nearly as friendly to me as the year before.'

By 1932, the Colonel was also having problems with Babe Didrikson. She wanted more money. 'Well, heck, it seems as though I'm gonna have to go somewhere else,' she said. 'I'm tired of working and giving them all this advertisement for nothing – $90.00 a month, it's terrible – I've told them I was gonna leave but they don't seem to think I know what I'm talking about.'

She went on unofficial strike. 'I'm sitting on the bench most of the game now because I won't try to play ball – I play about a half or more and won't make a shot. I miss every one of them cause I don't want to play with them for nothing.'

Colonel McCombs waited her out. By the end of the season, the Golden Cyclones were runners-up again in the national basketball championship. Babe was again named an All-American. She quit, though, a few weeks before the 1932 national track and field athletics championships, which that year were also the Olympic trials. She wanted some extra paid vacation time, but the company held firm. Colonel McCombs reminded her that the insurance company was flying her to Illinois to the Olympic trials, and paying for everything right through to the Olympics. That amounted, he said, to a six-week holiday.

Unhappy but up against the wall, Didrikson tearfully returned. By the time she arrived at the trials in Evanston, Illinois, though, she was all braggadocio. She raised hackles by saying – in more words but with no modesty, girlish or otherwise – that she was the greatest. People knew from her record that she was good. She was allowed to compete in as many events as she liked. 'Oh, we were mad,' said Hall, 'because we had always been limited to three events' – and they still would be at the actual Olympics. Babe entered eight events. Her victories in more events than she would be allowed to compete in at the Olympics would eliminate other women from competing at the Games.

Hall recalls, 'They'd hold up an event to wait for her and let her rest from the last one. She had such advantages, and she acted as if the world owed it all to her. I didn't like Babe anymore. The childish girl I had met in Dallas in 1930 was gone. She had been so nice then.'

Part of this rancour surely is jealousy. Part of it is a clash of culture and class. Texas rednecks thought it good form to brag about their exploits; so did Norse heroes. For nice middle-class girls modesty was the virtue.

Babe Didrikson was not a nice middle-class girl. She was a down-home Texan, Huck Finn with muscle and breasts. She kept bragging that she was going to win everything. She did too, placing in all but one of her events and scoring thirty points, eight more than the runner-up, Illinois Women's Athletic Club, which had twenty-two players.

But the confidence Babe exuded was phoney. The night before the competition she developed severe stomach pains and other classic anxiety symptoms. The hotel doctor, summoned at dawn, said it was just nerves. Babe slept hardly at all that night, falling asleep after daybreak. She and her chaperone Mrs Henry Wood overslept and dashed to Dyche Stadium by taxi with so little time to spare that Babe changed into her track clothes under a blanket in the back seat.

Weak and tired, that Saturday, 16 July, she went out on to the field. Her throw of 139 feet 3 inches broke her own world javelin record by six feet. She won in the shot put with a throw of 39 feet 6¼ inches, and came fourth in the discus. Then she threw a baseball 272 feet 2 inches – an excellent throw but nowhere near her best of 313 feet. Her leap of 17 feet 6⅝ inches won the long jump. Her run of 12.1 seconds won the 80-metre hurdles – she beat Evelyne Hall in the finals. Then she tied with Jean Shiley for a new high-jump world record.

'It was one of those days when you know you could fly'

Babe Didrikson

The tally in eight events was five victories, a tie and two world records. All in three hours, a single afternoon. Not even the most purple-prosed sportswriter could do the day justice. The UPI wire service reporter, whose report would be read in newspapers across the nation, called it 'the most amazing series of performances ever accomplished by any individual, male or female, in track and field history'. Most of the sportswriters waxed poetic. One headline did say, 'Babe Breaks Records Easier Than Dishes.' Babe Didrikson didn't mind a lot. She played golf with the sportswriters; you could also say she 'played ball'. She agreed with them that she, Babe, was the greatest, and that was more important than that she be modest or demure. Most of them loved the Babe more even than Evelyne Hall and Jean Shiley disliked her.

Babe Didrikson herself seems to have given little thought to Hall or Shiley or any other of her tight-lipped opponents and their sense of outraged middle-class propriety. Like the stomach pains and that anxious, sleepless night, they counted for nothing when she got into the stadium. She remembered the joy: 'It was one of those days in an athlete's life when you know you're just right,' she said. 'You feel you could fly. You're like a feather floating in the air.'

Then came the 1932 Olympics, at Los Angeles.

There were 1,408 athletes, 127 of them women, from thirty-seven countries. The American team had made the westward journey by train, in a red, white and blue banner-decked private railway car. By the time they arrived in Los Angeles, Evelyne Hall had had quite enough of Mildred Didrikson. 'She delighted in yanking the pillow out from under your head when you were asleep. She and Gloria Russell, a javelin competitor, also used to throw pillows at the girls. They especially liked to throw them at girls who wouldn't retaliate. We had feathers all over the car,' Hall says. 'She also used to take ice from the water cooler and drop it down our backs.'

Los Angeles boasted the first-ever specially built Olympic Village. It was for the men. Strict rules against women in the village barred the Finnish team's female cook. The women athletes were put up at the Chapman Park Hotel.

But in the press, they got the full Hollywood treatment. They were glamorous Olympic starlets. Even before the Games officially opened, Babe Didrikson was asked to reveal her 'beauty diet': 'I eat anything I want – except greasy foods and gravy. I pass the gravy. That's just hot grease anyway, with some flour and water in it.'

The *New York Times* broached the subject of feminine pursuits: 'Naturally athletics have not left me much time for household tasks for which a girl is supposed to have some liking, but I do not care about them. If necessary, however, I can sew and cook. One of my dresses won first place in a Texas State contest in 1930.'

Not that it mattered much to the sportswriters, who cared more about world records than hems. To be sure, she was presented as an oddity, a phenomenon, a kind of lovable freak, but not a great deal more so than they would have presented a male athlete whose abilities were equally exceptional. The boys of the press felt at ease with her. They liked her manly honesty. They shared her obsession with sports. They called her the Terrific Tomboy or the Texas Tornado or Whatta-Gal.

'I came out here to beat everybody in sight, and that is exactly what I'm going to do,' Babe said. 'Sure I can do anything.'[3] It was good copy.

'How many world records are you going to break?' a journalist asked.

'I'd break 'em all if they'd let me,' she said. It was duly reported.

The Depression was still on, but the Olympic organizers had gone in for plenty of razzmatazz. They would, like their counterparts half a century later, make a nice profit. No previous Olympics had made money; Los Angeles would garner more than a million dollars.

President Hoover did not attend the opening of the Tenth Olympiad – only two days before, his troops had fired at the bonus marchers in Washington, DC, killing one man. Two babies died of tear-gas fumes. Some said Hoover was scared to show his face; some said he was too busy. The Vice President did the Olympic honours on hot, humid 30 July. Every seat in the Coliseum had been sold. A reverent crowd of 105,000 – the largest ever to attend the Olympics – was there for the two-hour opening ceremony. A robed chorus sang 'The Star-Spangled Banner', doves flew, the athletes intoned the Olympic oath. Reporters spoke of an awesome occasion.

'To tell you the truth, I couldn't enjoy the ceremonies that much after we all got out there,' Babe Didrikson said. 'We all had to wear special dresses and stockings and white shoes that the Olympic Committee had issued us. I believe it was about the first time I'd ever worn a pair of stockings in my life; I was used to anklets and socks. As for the shoes they were really hurting my feet.' During the ceremony, she took them off.

The next afternoon, fifty thousand people watched as, on her first throw, she broke the javelin record by more than four feet. The crowd cheered her 43.68 metre (143 foot 4 inch) throw.[4] Babe clasped her hands over her head in a gesture of victory. It had been

Below: **Babe Didrikson, nearest the camera, winning the hurdles and *opposite:* on the rostrum with Evelyne Hall and Marjorie Clark**

an odd flight of the javelin. Instead of soaring, it had been straight and low. There was talk of a snazzy new technique. Babe burst that pretentious bubble too. 'My hand slipped when I picked up the pole. It slid along about six inches and then I got a good grip again. And then I threw it and it just went.'

She had torn some cartilage in her shoulder on that wrenching throw, but it didn't matter. She had won. And, since Olympic rules limited her to entering only three events, her remaining two were the hurdles and the high jump, where leg muscles were what counted.

Two days later, in the 80-metre hurdles, her main rival was again Evelyne Hall. Hall got the better start, but Babe took each hurdle in three long strides compared to Hall's four. There were seven hurdles, each 2 feet 6 inches high. Both women jumped well, and they were soon leg to leg in world-record time. As she crossed the finish line, Babe called out to Evelyne Hall, 'Well, I won again.' Years later, Hall insisted she got a welt on her neck from breaking the tape. Both were credited with the 11.7 second world mark, but the new photo-finish equipment had to be consulted to decide the winner. The judges and the photo awarded the gold medal to Babe Didrikson.

On the last day of the Games came the high jump. Didrikson told the press: 'Yep, I'm going to win the high jump Sunday and set a world record. I don't know who my opponents are and, anyways, it wouldn't make any difference. I hope they are good.'

The field was well known and splendid. Carolina Gisolf, of Holland, had previously held the world record. And there was also Jean Shiley, the same Jean Shiley with whom Babe had tied at the trials two weeks earlier. Shiley, a tall, angular woman with brown hair, was the captain of the American team. Babe Didrikson had also been nominated for the post. A third nominee, friendly to Shiley, had withdrawn, lest in a threeway split the Babe should win.

Shiley didn't like Didrikson's manner or manners. The two women also had utterly different jumping styles. Babe Didrikson dived (the Western roll) and Shiley used the – then conventional but today rare – scissors jump. The competition was tense and had a few surprises. Carolina Gisolf failed her jump and went out at 5 feet 2¼ inches. The Canadian Eva Dawes went out at 5 feet 3. Didrikson and Shiley were the only two left in the competition when the bar went up to 5 feet 5¼ inches. That was 1.65 metres. Whoever cleared the bar at that height would set a new world record. Both women made clean jumps. The bar went up an inch. Babe cleared it, but on landing she kicked one of the uprights and the bar fell. The judges ruled no jump. Shiley failed too. The bar went down an inch. Both jumpers cleared it. Should they share the gold medal?

The judges broke the deadlock with an astonishingly illogical decision. They declared that both would share the world record, but because Didrikson had dived on her last jump, it was illegal. Shiley was therefore the winner; Didrikson the silver medalist. But Babe Didrikson had been using the same method of jumping throughout the competition. It was a quirky, indeed a bizarre decision – an illegal jump ought to be disqualified, not awarded a world record; and it ought to be pointed out early in the competition, not at the end.

Jean Shiley said, 'The other girls on the team were delighted, like children at Christmas because I had beaten Babe.'

The judges had ruled against Babe Didrikson twice in the high-jump competition. 'For the first time since I've been in athletics I am a bit mixed up,' she said. 'I am all twisted . . . I jumped in all parts of the United States before some of the best judges in the country and they all approved that method and even the judges out there Sunday afternoon had nothing to say about it until I had twice cleanly cleared the bar.' The Olympic judges were not above reproach.

Even without the third gold medal, Babe Didrikson was acclaimed from the Atlantic to the Pacific as an Olympic heroine. She was called 'the greatest athlete of all mankind for all time'. She was described as 'the most flawless section of muscle harmony, of complete mental and physical coordination the world of sport has ever known'. No one had ever before won medals in throwing, running and jumping events – and she had set records in all three events. Employers Casualty put her on a plane to Dallas. She was greeted with 'Hail to the Chief'. The Golden Cyclones flanked the fire chief's red limousine where Babe was perched amid the red roses. 'Come on up here! Come on!' she shouted to her sister Lillie when she saw her in the crowd. And they rode together in the parade through Dallas. There were streamers and confetti and cheers.

The Didriksen family had had two flat tyres on the way from Beaumont. 'The big shots, they was all lookin' at us country folks,' Lillie said. 'But we didn't care. Babe didn't care. Babe had to buy us

'The other girls were delighted because I had beaten Babe'

High Jumper Jean Shiley

'I have lost but I wasn't beaten'

Babe Didrikson

31

'The most amazing series of performances ever accomplished by male or female'

United Press International, 1932

some tyres to get us back to Beaumont that day.' It was two and a half years since Babe herself had left Beaumont to become a Dallas Cyclone. In Dallas, the celebrations lasted two days, and then Babe flew home to Beaumont for another parade in another fire chief's car.

Soon, her status as an amateur athlete began to be questioned. Supposedly, she was still earning $90 a month, and she was driving an $835 Dodge car. When she said she was paying it off at $69 a month, officials wondered how she could afford to buy food. Wasn't the car an illegal gift? Then Babe's photograph appeared in a Dodge newspaper advertisement. She lost her amateur status and the right to play for the Golden Cyclones. Eventually, it was 'proved' that the endorsement had appeared without her knowledge. She was reinstated. In Detroit, she made daily appearances at the Auto Show, signing autographs at the Dodge stand. Clearly, she *was* going professional. She needed the money. All of the Didriksen family did.

In Chicago, she did an eighteen-minute vaudeville act in which, among other things, she played the harmonica. The newspapers were kind; the audiences flocked in; there were big contracts looming. She quit: 'I want to live my life outdoors,' she said. 'I want to play golf.'

Meanwhile, she played a little professional baseball. In Brooklyn, she got $400 for forty minutes play. In the autumn of 1933, Babe Didrikson's All-Americans, a basketball team of men and women, began a hectic five-month tour, playing against small-town teams in the Middle West and on the Eastern seaboard. In the Depression-struck farm communities, in the drab mill towns, thousands of people paid to see Babe Didrikson. The All-Americans went from Iowa to Missouri, Kansas, Nebraska, South Dakota, Minnesota, Wisconsin, Illinois, Michigan, Ohio, Pennsylvania, New York, Vermont, Massachusetts, New Hampshire, New Jersey and Connecticut. At a time when garment-workers were earning $2.39 for a fifty-hour week, Babe Didrikson was paid $1000 a month, more than $250 a week. A teammate says she converted the money into large bills and sent them home to Beaumont by post until the team convinced her it was safer to buy money orders. Over nearly four years, making appearances in this sport and that, she earned about $40,000. Good money, but it had no cachet; it was thought of as shoddy work. There was something demeaning about being paid for sport, especially if you were a woman. A good woman would have a man to support her. Why did she need to work?

The reaction set in. In college gyms, signs on the bulletin boards soon warned young women against becoming 'muscle molls'. Babe was a Muscle Moll. A quarter of a century later, the same jibe would be used against the Australian swimmer Dawn Fraser, who disdained frills, and against others. Many women would avoid sport in order to avoid a butch image. Now mothers – and not just in Beaumont, Texas – said to their daughters, 'Don't be like the Babe.' Mascara, the message went, was more suitable for women than muscle.

In 1938, to the relief of many, Babe Didrikson got married. He was a wrestler, 400-pound George Zaharias. He thought her a slip of a thing.

Now she was becoming a prominent golfer. She had tackled golf the same way she tackled athletics: 'For nearly four months I hit golf balls from early morning until late afternoon – hit balls until tape was piled on top of tape covering the blisters and cracks in my hands. Then I entered my first tournament, the 1935 Texas Women's Championship at Houston, and won.'[5] Eventually, Babe Didrikson became the finest and the most famous woman golfer of her generation. Some of the country-club set tried to keep her out of the game, but Didrikson found allies. She beat every other woman on the golf tour. She even beat Katherine Hepburn at golf in the movie *Pat and Mike.*

When he was US President, Didrikson Zaharias's golfing chum Dwight David Eisenhower spoke of the military-industrial complex. It was the first time that the joint enterprise of the armed forces and industry had been given a name. Mildred Didrikson Zaharias was backed by what has yet to be named but most surely is recognizable as the sports-industrial complex. There was always Big Money behind her big talent. Her brash talk would not, in this post-Mohammed Ali era, shock many today. Neither would the money she made from sport. After decades of shoddy, under-the-table money, shamateurism is largely over; Olympic athletes are now allowed to earn money from sport.

Didrikson was unashamed of her physical prowess. Her unselfconsciousness enabled her to use her physical prowess to the full. In this she was a pioneer, voicing a woman's right to be strong, able, to show mastery in sport. She was the sort of woman who took off tight shoes which hurt and wiggled her toes, no matter where she was. She had respect for her body. To please her chaperone though, she did wear a frilly pink hat on occasion. Some saw her as a freak; others as a phenomenon. She was a star.

It was ironic that so straightforward a person should have image problems. Babe Didrikson was the first athlete to make people confront issues of femininity: how much muscle is too much? how much is unfeminine? Didrikson lacked the sophistication to pretend she liked crinolines and hair curlers. She showed off her rippling muscles. She was down-home, earthy, able.

When she got to be a golf star, a friend convinced her that some glamour was necessary. The new Babe Didrikson Zaharias had long hair and wore bright red nail polish. She had always been, and still was, an exquisite athlete.

During her career, she set nineteen records in track and field. She is still the only athlete in Olympic history to win individual running, jumping and throwing events.

Unlike Babe Didrikson, Jackie Joyner-Kersee seems shy. Or perhaps the greatest all-round woman athlete of our era is just too tired from training to want to chat much. It is her coach and husband Bob Kersee who usually answers the questions you put. But when Joyner-Kersee was asked by NBC Television to name the athlete she would most like to be, she answered for herself, choosing Babe Didrikson: 'I saw a story about her on TV [when I was] a kid. I sure wish I could take her arm and put it on mine.'

Five-foot ten-inch tall, 153-pound Jackie Joyner-Kersee, who lives in California, became the world champion heptathlete in 1987. The heptathlon, first included in the Olympics in 1984, is an all-round track and field event for women. It takes place over two gruelling days. Day one consists of 100-metres hurdles, the high jump, shot and the 200-metres sprint; day two, the long jump, javelin, and the 800 metres. Points are awarded for each of the seven events. If Babe Didrikson were competing today, she would probably be a heptathlete.

In 1984, fifty-two years after Didrikson's triumph in Los Angeles, the first Olympic heptathlon took place in the same city. Joyner-Kersee had an off-day, because her hamstrings were hurting more than usual, and she lost by five points to the Australian Glynis Nunn. Those five points meant silver instead of gold and must have been hateful when the score was 6,390 points to 6,385.

Since then Joyner-Kersee has broken her sport's psychological barrier by becoming the first woman to score over 7,000 points. By

'My main opponent is Wilhelmina World Record'

Jackie Joyner-Kersee

the close of 1987, she had achieved the event's four highest scores. Her standard was so much higher than any other heptathlete's that the only rival she had was her own world record. 'Jackie's got to think of the world record as another competitor,' Bob Kersee said. 'I've named it Wilhelmina World Record.'[6]

Wilhelmina beat her in Rome that September at the world athletics championships, but Joyner-Kersee, then twenty-five, beat everybody else, winning the world title. In Rome, she also competed in the individual long jump, picking up the world record,

Heike Drechsler

defeating the only other woman who could claim to be the world's greatest track and field athlete, Heike Drechsler. The twenty-three-year-old East German was not a heptathlete, but competed instead in the individual events. She had arrived at the world championships as the world record-holder at 200 metres and in the long jump.

Drechsler's knee was aching. She had injured it on the first jump and, after the fourth, it was so painful she didn't take the last two jumps. As she listened to the American national anthem, 'The Star Spangled Banner', being played by the world championship orchestra in Rome, she stood on the victory platform in the unfamiliar bronze medal position. She and Joyner-Kersee were now joint holders of the 7.45-metre world long-jump record.

Joyner-Kersee, standing on the higher gold medal-winner's platform, towered above Drechsler, although she is an inch shorter. Jackie Joyner-Kersee was enjoying her victory, but she was looking forward to icing her perennially aching hamstrings. Joyner-Kersee may have the strongest fast-twitch muscles in sport; but she has tight, fragile hamstrings. Even if both athletes defeat Wilhelmina a few more times, both will probably eventually be defeated by the nemesis of these aching sinews.

When 'The Star Spangled Banner' was over, Heike Drechsler patted Joyner-Kersee on the shoulder. 'You're the best,' Drechsler said. The two women embraced.

'We both', Joyner-Kersee remembers, 'had tears in our eyes. For her to say that really made me feel good.'

Olympic opening ceremony, Berlin, 1936

CHAPTER 3

NAZI FOIL

The Führer, in army uniform, strode across the crowded, expectant Olympic stadium. It was he who would declare the Games officially open. He paused to accept a bouquet of flowers from the five-year-old girl whose father had planned the Games. Then, as the Olympic orchestra played Wagner's resounding 'March of Homage', Adolph Hitler took his place in the box of honour. Beside him stood Goebbels, dressed in crisp white, and Hesse.

Above the stadium, the largest Zeppelin airship in the world, with huge swastika markings on its tail-fins, hovered in the grey sky. The 900-foot long, 160-foot wide Zeppelin was towing the Olympic flag. Throughout the Olympic city, the Nazi presence could be felt. Swastikas forty-five feet high towered over Berlin's famous Unter den Linden boulevard. Men and boys parading starchily in uniform – soldiers, sailors, airmen, brown-shirted Hitler Youth – seemed to be everywhere. Thousands of girls in white uniform, the *Bund Deutscher Mädchen*, stood at attention in the Lustgarten at the youth festival that preceded the opening of the Games. Soldiers lined the route to the Olympic stadium. The rumours that the 1936 Berlin Games were to be a showcase of Nazi military might were proving all too true.

The 4,066 athletes – 328 of them women – marched into the stadium in procession, nation by nation. Last came the German team, clad entirely in white. Among them was the champion fencer Hélène Mayer, who was known to be half Jewish. As the German team marched into the centre of the Olympic stadium, the crowd rose to its feet and a hundred thousand arms went up in the Nazi salute.

Without a doubt, Hélène Mayer's situation was anomalous. She had returned from the safety of California to rabidly anti-Semitic Germany in order to compete at these Olympics. She was a former Olympic champion, and she was typically Aryan in appearance – blonde, statuesque, five foot ten inches tall. Her fans had called her 'Die blonde Hé'. But because she was 'tainted' with Jewish blood, she had been dropped from her German fencing club. The American general who had lobbied to get her reinstated on the German Olympic team had had his own reasons. The fact that Hélène Mayer was to compete for Germany at the Nazi Olympics was in itself an achievement. Whether or not it was a commendable achievement is still a controversial question.

Hitler took the microphone to declare the Eleventh Olympiad of the modern era open. Canons boomed. The twenty thousand carrier pigeons released into the stadium disappeared into the leaden Berlin sky. The composer Richard Strauss led the orchestra in his own Olympic Hymn. The bearer of the Olympic torch ran into the stadium to set alight the Olympic flame.

Below: **German ladies team;** *opposite:* **Hélène Mayer**

'Germany in every way [is] living up to the Olympic rules'

Count Baillet-Latour, chairman IOC, 1935

The International Olympic Committee had been eager to have Jewish athletes on the German team to dispel charges that in allowing the Olympics to go ahead in Berlin, the IOC was acceding to racism. Hélène Mayer was a hard-won token. Prejudice against 'non-Aryans', particularly Jews, had already become violent and was increasingly nasty in Germany. In 1933, six months after Hitler came to power, the Minister of Education barred Jews from youth groups. Non-Aryan athletes were barred from training sessions, dropped from clubs, denied coaching.

Two years later, the Nuremberg Laws made it clear that Jews and those of 'mixed blood' no longer qualified to be German citizens. Nor could any non-Aryan athletes represent Germany. The tennis player Danny Prenn, a German Jew, had been dropped from the Davis Cup team. Non-Aryan visitors to Germany suffered too. The wrestler Jim Wango, who was black, had died because doctors in Nuremberg refused to treat him.

Those who were appalled at the Nazis' behaviour thought it hypocritical to stage the Olympics in Germany. In the United States, the Amateur Athletic Union, which ran the sport, had received more than a hundred thousand protests from individuals against American participation in the Games. Later, the AAU itself would formally request withdrawal. The IOC had long been urged to move the Olympics and now that it was too late many people thought the only decent thing was to boycott the Nazi Olympics.

In the autumn of 1935, General Charles Sherrill, one of the three American members of the International Olympic Committee, visited Germany. The result was that two German Jewish athletes, Hélène Mayer and the high jumper Gretel Bergmann, who had settled in England, were invited to return from exile to compete for Germany.

'No admittance to Jews'

Ski club poster at Garmisch-Partenkirchen, removed for the 1936 Winter Olympics

Encouraged by IOC representatives, both athletes accepted the offer. Perhaps they thought the best argument they could make against 'Aryan supremacy' was to go to the Games and win. Perhaps it was just that the Olympics are the summit of sport, and as athletes, both women wanted terribly to be there. Even after General Sherrill returned from Berlin, there were protests and a formal request for a boycott from the AAU, but the 'concession' Sherrill had won – he said after two years of wrangling – swayed the balance. By gaining a place for these two athletes on the German team, the American general saved the Nazi Olympics.

The Nazis welched on their agreement to field the high jumper,

Gretel Bergmann. Bergmann, who had become the English high-jump champion in 1934, went to Germany as planned. Her name was listed on the Olympic programme as a member of the German team. There are reports that at the Olympic trials she cleared an impressive 1.64 metres, 10 cm. higher than the next woman jumped. But a letter came claiming that her standard was insufficient for the Games. Perhaps because the British did not seem too awfully concerned, she would not be allowed to compete. It was to be a Hungarian, Ibolya Csak, who would win the gold medal, with a jump of 1.60 metres.

Hélène Mayer, with America's eyes watching, fared better. Mayer was regarded as the finest fencing stylist in the world. She had had her first lesson when a child in Offenbach, and at just thirteen she won the German foil championship. In 1928, still only seventeen, she won the Olympic gold medal in the foil. In 1929 and 1931, she was the world foil champion. At the Los Angeles Olympics in 1932, she again competed for Germany but she was ill and came fifth.

Hélène Mayer decided to stay on in California to study international law at the University of Southern California. Soon afterwards she changed her field of study to languages. In 1933, as anti-Semitic laws took hold in Germany, she was expelled *in absentia* from her home fencing club. The following year and the year after that, she entered the American national foil championships and won.

When the offer came late in 1935 to compete for Germany, she was living in California, teaching languages. Her father, Dr Ludwig Mayer, who died in 1931, had been Jewish. Her mother and two brothers still lived in Germany. It is not known for certain whether she was raised as a Jew or a Christian. When the politically aware Rabbi Stephen Wise of New York urged Mayer to stay home in the United States, she told him to mind his own business. Hers was fencing, and where better to do it than at the Olympics?

Although Mayer – like hockey player Rudi Ball, who returned from exile in France – jumped at the chance to compete for Germany, some of the famous Jewish athletes who lived in other countries chose to boycott Berlin. The bobsled champion Philippe de Rothschild and the male fencer Jean Rheims stayed in France. Nor did the Austrian swimmer Judith Deutsch go.

The ampitheatre where the Olympic foil competition was taking place was packed. They had all come to see Hélène Mayer, who

> **'The tension of competition was shot through with an undercurrent of race [and] politics'**
>
> **Richard D Mandell,** *The Nazi Olympics*

some were surprised to see looked like any other *Fraülein*, with her flaxen hair braided and pulled around her head. Three of the greatest fencers of modern times were there – the reigning Olympic champion Ellen Preis, an Austrian; an ageing newcomer from Hungary, Ilona Schacherer-Elek, who was Jewish, and Mayer herself. All three had survived the elimination matches, and were among the eight women who were to face each other in the finals. The winner would be decided on overall points rather than on the outcome of any one match. Tension was high. The crowd was warned to be silent.

There was no sound as Mayer, who towered over Elek, lunged at her in the first of their encounters. Ilona Elek was small but quick, a left-hander. She had none of Mayer's classic style, and she had a shorter reach, but she was an excellent strategist. The crowd was willing her to lose. But Elek fought on. Playing to Mayer's weaknesses, she won their three bouts, 3 to 2, 4 to 4 and 5 to 4. But only time would tell who would eventually be Olympic champion.

Mayer fenced on, besting all her other opponents including every Aryan she faced. Mayer, it seemed, must be ahead on points.

Now came the most dramatic match of the Games. Mayer versus the reigning Olympic champion, the Austrian 'Aryan' Preis. Mayer lunged; an agile Ellen Preis dodged. Preis lunged; big Hélène Mayer eluded her with uncanny agility. Their match which evoked such rapt attention ended in a draw: 2 to 2, 3 to 3, 4 to 4.

Who would be the new champion? The officials added up the points all eight women in the finals had scored. Preis was, to the dismay of many, only the bronze medalist. Hélène Mayer had to be satisfied with silver. Perhaps being an international *cause célèbre* had taken some toll. The winner: Ilona Schacherer-Elek, at twenty-nine, the oldest woman gold medalist at the 1936 Games. She would make further Olympic history by winning gold again in 1948 and silver in 1952 when she was forty-five. In Berlin, in 1936, few were delighted that she, a 'non-Aryan', had won.

The victory ceremony was held in the Olympic stadium. The three women mounted the dais and the medals were placed around their necks. As the anthem played, Hélène Mayer, who had been born and reared in Germany, who felt German even though she had been stripped of her citizenship, raised her right arm in the Heil Hitler salute.

The crowd in the Berlin stadium roared its approval. The rest of the world had quite another reaction.

'The burning question was whether to salute Hitler or not'

Dorothy Odam Tyler, high jump silver medallist

After the Olympics, Hélène Mayer, who could never be a German citizen despite any show of fealty, went home to California. In 1937 she defeated the Olympic champion Ilona Elek at the world championships, but never again competed internationally. In her adopted country, Hélène Mayer continued to compete in the national championships. She had won the American title twice before the Olympics. After the Games, she won it another half dozen times.

Crowd pleaser: Ellen Preis, Ilona Elek and Hélène Mayer giving the Nazi salute

The 1936 Olympics were recorded in a brilliant but pro-Reich documentary movie, *Olympische Spiele*, made by the female director, Leni Riefenstahl. Neither the half-Jewish fencer who became a pawn of Nazidom, nor the Hungarian Jew who defeated her, figures large.

CHAPTER 4

MOTHERS RUN BEST

*B*omb-scarred London, 1948. There were pools of water on the cinder track. Fanny Blankers-Koen huddled under the umbrella that Jan held over her, and waited for the race to begin. Because of the war, these were the first Olympics since 1936. Jan Blankers, her coach, for eight years now also her husband, had found ways for her to train throughout the Nazi occupation of Holland. She had continued to run, even though there was never enough of anything, including time and food and freedom.

Now she intended to make all those hard years count. No matter what the cynical journalists and the belligerent British team manager had said about her, she intended to win this race. She was not too old. And it did not matter (and no one knew) that she was three months pregnant.

The war had been over just three years. Children in London were still playing on bomb sites. Food and clothing were rationed. As in Europe, coal was scarce. So were pots and pans and places to live. The only things there were plenty of in Olympic London were rain and shortages. These were the Ration Book Games. There was no special Olympic Village; visiting athletes were billeted here and there. She and the other Dutch women were staying at St Helen's School, Northwood. But the beds were comfortable enough. They had lived through six years of war in occupied Holland – the makeshift accommodation wasn't what was troubling Fanny Blankers-Koen.

Nor was the weather, which had been blistering yesterday and today was transforming the temporary track, laid for the duration of the Games in the Wembley stadium, into a canal. But Holland was not a dry country either. She had often run in the rain. And she was

Fanny Blankers-Koen after the hurdles race, London, 1948. It was still raining!

beginning to be fond of post-Blitzkrieg London. There were all the discomforts of home.

How different these Games were from the lavish, intimidating splendour she had seen at the Hitler Olympics, of which she did not have fond memories. The Dutch heroine there had been Hendrika Mastenbroek, who won four swimming medals, three of them gold. 'Rie' Mastenbroek was seventeen, exactly ten months younger than the then Francina 'Fanny' Koen, who had consoled herself with the hope that she was going to be a late bloomer.

Then the war had stolen her best Olympic years. But she would show them anyway. Yes, she *was* old, three months past thirty. But she was not *too* old. Yes, she was a 'blonde-haired mother of two'. Little Jan was seven; little Fanny three. And there was a third baby on the way. But their mother was far from ready to slow down. It wasn't vanity that was motivating her: she wasn't mutton trying to parade as lamb. It was the desire to achieve what she was capable of, the will to win.

But could a woman whose body had endured pregnancy and birth still be strong enough to prevail at the Olympics? Could a woman over thirty win an Olympic sprint final? Most people thought not.

Yet, if anything, bearing two children had made her faster. Even without the spur of being able to compete against the world's best in the flesh, in 1942 – the year after their son's birth – she had run the 80 metres hurdles in 11.3 seconds, equalling the world record. In 1943, fully fit again, she bettered two world records, with a long jump of 6.25 metres and a high jump of 1.71 metres. Each time she wheeled the baby carriage into the stadium, set it by the track and laced up her running shoes, each time she practised one of the jumps, she yearned for the war to be over. For peace which would bring the Olympics. Was that so selfish? In 1944 she ran the 100 yard dash in 10.8 seconds, again shattering the world record, and she was a member of the world record breaking team in two relay events, 4 × 110 yards and 4 × 200 metres.

Her daughter was born in 1945, too close to the European championships in Oslo to allow her to set any new world records. She did, though, win gold medals there at 80 metres hurdles and in the 4 × 100 metres relay. In 1945, at the end of the war, she set a world 100-metres record, of 11.5 seconds.

But now was it too late? The British team manager Jack Crump was not alone in regarding a woman past thirty as old. Few women her age would find it appealing – or appropriate – to run round an athletics track. Most wouldn't, indeed couldn't, even run for a tram or a bus. Nor, ironically, would they want to do anything so aggressive as compete. In the Second World War, women had flown planes and – seemingly – the coop. For many, parental and husbandly authority vanished for the duration, as women became riveters, ambulance drivers, spies. In Holland, little girls knew how to lie convincingly about the whereabouts of their fathers when questioned by Nazi officers. During the long years of warfare, women not only learned they had muscle, they had been relied on to use it. But now the war was over. The men were home and wanted their jobs back; they wanted their women back in the kitchen too. They didn't want back-talk. And women were told that all that responsibility they had had to shoulder, all that freedom, was unwomanly, unnatural.

Fanny Blankers-Koen knew she was fortunate. The men in her life were different. Her husband was encouraging her to stretch her limits. Her father was the one who had first noticed her gift for sport. He took her to the coach Jan Blankers, and saw no reason why she shouldn't bicycle eighteen miles to the track.

And even if he had, he couldn't have kept her away. She loved sport long before she loved Jan Blankers. Together they had worked to arrive, at last, at this Olympics, where she was entering four of the nine women's track and field events. Four was the maximum allowed. She had decided that in her circumstances it was best to omit the long jump and the high jump, even though she still held both world records.

The minutes till the 100-metres race ticked on the clock. She had already won her heat and the semi-final. Now it was time for the final. She had been waiting for twelve years for the coming eleven or twelve seconds on the Olympic track. Would she, could she, win the gold medal?

They were under starter's orders. The 100 metres is a matter of pure speed. Of all the running events, it is the briefest. Because the distance is so short, the pace is faster than in any other event. On the clock, the winner is the fastest woman in the world.

At the sound of the starter's pistol, Fanny Blankers-Koen in her bright, baggy orange shorts and white shirt, the traditional Dutch colours, surged forward. So did the others. In 11.9 seconds it was over. And just as Fanny Blankers-Koen had almost known it would, her long stride carried her over the sodden cinders to victory. Fully a metre (three yards) behind came Dorothy Manley of Britain, who finished second in 12.2 seconds. The Australian Shirley Strickland, credited with an identical time, was placed third. Fanny Blankers-Koen had her first gold medal of the Games.

The worst was still to come: the 80-metres hurdles race. Blankers-Koen's knees shook at the thought. True, she was the world record holder. True, too, only the day before she had achieved her great ambition: she was an Olympic gold medalist at last. But surely no one could ever have felt less like a champion than she did on that Tuesday morning, the day of the hurdles heats. She had never ever been so nervous before a race.

Jan Blankers was nervous too. 'You must concentrate', he said, 'because this English girl knows her business.'[1] The English 'girl', Maureen Gardner, was nineteen.

Blankers-Koen had never seen or met Gardner, but she knew she had a fast time of 11.2 seconds in the hurdles. Blankers-Koen's best time, set earlier in the year, was better, 11.0. But even in Holland they had heard that this young Gardner had accomplished much with her new coach. Who knew what she would be capable of before a British crowd in Britain at the Olympics?

And when Gardner arrived, by car, with her own set of hurdles so that she could get in some training before the heats, Blankers-Koen's anxiety level increased. Only a very serious and knowledgeable athlete would travel with her own hurdles. It didn't occur to her then that maybe a British hurdler would have been warned that at the Ration Book Games there would be no spare hurdles. When, after a while, Blankers-Koen walked over to Gardner, shook hands, and asked to borrow the hurdles, she noticed Gardner was just as nervous as she was. The practice helped. Blankers-Koen won her heat and her semi-final, but was taken aback by how good Maureen Gardner looked, and how even though she had had a bad semi-final, scraping a hurdle and losing her balance, she still managed to achieve third and a place in the final. What would happen when Gardner had a good race? Blankers-Koen's teammates told her, 'It will not be an easy win for you.'

The night before the 80-metres hurdles final, Fanny Blankers-Koen slept badly. She ran the race over and over in her mind. And she had a little dialogue with herself. One part of her said, consolingly, it didn't matter if she lost. Since 1936, she had wanted to be an Olympic champion. And now she was. 'Be satisfied,' she told herself.

Another part of her said, 'Why be content? Maureen Gardner is no better than you are. Go out and win. Of course you can do it.'

In the morning Fanny Blankers-Koen was much too nervous to eat anything. She told Jan she had eaten, but she would have to run the race on an empty stomach. At half past one, she arrived at the track. It was another dull, dreary day. She changed, warmed up with limbering exercises and a jog round the track – and she waited. It was agony.

Just before the three o'clock start, Jan Blankers taunted her with the words, 'You are too old, Fanny.'

Those five words were spoken with a purpose. It wasn't cruelty. It was to remind her of what she had to prove to the people who had written her off. It was time now. She stripped off her warmups, smoothed her orange shorts, and checked that her number, 692, was pinned on securely. She had drawn lane one, the lane next to

'Too old was I? I would show them'

Fanny Blankers-Koen

Maureen Gardner, and would be able to keep an eye on her. But the other woman in with a very good chance, Shirley Strickland, was at the other end of the track. Blankers-Koen would probably not have a moment spare during the race to crane her neck and see where Strickland was. She would have to trust to luck.

The crowd would be rooting for Gardner. She could sense they were full of expectation. Even King George VI and Queen Elizabeth were coming. They were due to arrive at the stadium any moment. These thoughts were not helping. She must concentrate. Suddenly, before she expected it, the starter's pistol fired, and she, who was known for being so quick off the mark, was left standing. The rest of the field were a yard ahead of her. Her confidence cracked. 'What is a yard? What is a fraction of a second? Not much,' was her fleeting thought. 'But in a race of 80 metres it can mean the difference between defeat and victory. You are beaten, Fanny. You'll never catch them.' Perhaps she *was* too old. No, no she wasn't, she wouldn't allow herself to be. She raced after Maureen Gardner, hurdle after hurdle, sprinting as she had never sprinted before. She ran faster, faster, faster. By the time they reached the fifth hurdle, she was level with Gardner, but Fanny Blankers-Koen was going so fast that she went too close to the hurdle, hit it, and lost her balance. She staggered, her style went to pieces, but she kept running forward. It was a blur, it was terrible, it was wonderful. She sensed rather than felt the tape against her breast.

She had won.

Or had she? The band was playing 'God Save the King', the British national anthem. Maureen Gardner had been right beside her. Had the judges decided in a close race to award the British girl the decision in London? But no, it seemed there had been no decision yet. The judges were awaiting the photo to decide the finish. The band was welcoming the king and queen.

After a while, the victor's running number was put up. Six. Nine. Fanny Blankers-Koen jumped into the air. Then the two appeared on the board. She had won, but it had indeed been close. Her time of 11.2 seconds, a new Olympic record, was shared with Maureen Gardner, who was awarded the silver medal. Strickland, in the white, gold and green of Australia, won the bronze.

The *London Daily Graphic* reported Fanny Blankers-Koen's great victory, her second Olympic gold medal, like this: 'FASTEST WOMAN IN THE WORLD IS AN EXPERT COOK.' No one was gainsaying her victory: an Olympic double, two gold medals, were not a matter of opinion; they could not be denied. But the newspaper headline and article stressed her traditionally feminine roles. 'I shall train my two children to be athletes as well', said a smaller boldface headline. The article continued: 'But at home she is just an ordinary housewife. She is an expert cook and darns socks with artistry. *Her greatest love next to racing is housework*' (my italics).

This was by no means the worst of which the newspaper was capable. Racing was cited as Blankers-Koen's first priority. The silver medalist, Maureen Gardner of Oxford, who had so nearly won the race, was portrayed far more stereotypically: 'Maureen Gardner, the shyest girl at the Games, is more excited about September 11 than about her record-breaking run. It is her wedding day.'

No doubt Gardner was excited about the wedding. But surely not more excited, not at that moment. It was inaccurate reporting. Inappropriate too. It was a sign that the feminine mystique which Betty Friedan would give a name to two decades later was taking hold. If a woman insisted on doing something so unladylike as running, she had better also be a whizz at cooking and cleaning. And if she wasn't, the papers would make her out to be.

Blankers-Koen was even more full of self-doubt after the heats of her next event, the new 200-metres race. She had won her heat, but in the other heats, her time of 25.7 seconds had been bettered by four other runners. There was a good chance she might be beaten in the final. Should she withdraw? As soon as the word got out that she was considering withdrawing, the rumour went around that it was because she was missing her children.

It was time to warm up for the semi-final. But the anxiety she felt was almost paralysing. After her warm-up, which she felt had done her almost no good, she left the track, and went back to the massage table. There she broke into sobs. How could she run, she couldn't even stop crying?

When it was time for the semi-final race, she tried to pull herself together. She felt much better after the cry. If she was going to run, and she was, she would have to give it everything, even though the race was only a semi-final. She needed the confidence that would come of winning it. She took her place on the track, and when the start sounded she erupted out of the blocks like Vesuvius, finishing in 24.3 seconds, the fastest 200 metres of the Games so far by a full second. She had done it.

In the final, once again she was unbeatable. Her time was 24.4

'Fastest Woman in the World is an Expert Cook'

Daily Graphic, London, August 5, 1948

'1924 was
Nurmi's year;
1936
[belonged] to
Jesse Owens
and 1948 to
Fanny
Blankers-
Koen'

**Olympic champion
Harold Abrahams**

seconds, and she crossed the line fully seven metres ahead of second-placed Audrey Williamson of Britain. The battle had been won inside her head. It was Fanny Blankers-Koen's third gold medal of the Games.

On the last day of competition, Saturday, 7 August, Blankers-Koen – now known worldwide as the 'Flying Dutch Housewife' – ran the anchor leg in the 400-metres relay. When she took the baton from Gerda Van der Kade Koudjis, the Dutch were in third place. The Australians were winning the race. Shirley Strickland had run the first leg. Now her teammate Joyce King looked set to win. With her long stride, Blankers-Koen passed Canada's Patricia Jones, and with just ten metres to go, she came level with Joyce King. Then, amazingly, Blankers-Koen accelerated and passed King. The Dutch won in 47.5 seconds, just a tenth of a second ahead of the Australians. Canada was but a tenth of a second behind them. It was a fourth gold medal for Fanny Blankers-Koen.

Many in the crowd stood to cheer her. The ration books and the rain were forgotten. She had entered four events and she had won them all. She had won every heat, every semi-final she had entered too. No woman had ever before won four gold medals.

She returned to Holland to a heroine's welcome. But not to retirement. In 1950, Fanny Blankers-Koen added the 220 yards world record to her list of sporting accomplishments, and at the European Championships, she won gold medals at 100 metres, 200 metres and at 80 metres hurdles. In 1951, at the age of thirty-three, she set yet another world record, in the pentathlon.

Forty years later, her total of four athletics golds has been equalled (by the Australian Betty Cuthbert in 1956 and 1964, and by the East German Barbel Eckert Wockel in 1976 and 1980). But her total is still a female record for a single Games.

Fanny Blankers-Koen was the most impressive Olympic athlete of her era. And she was the first of the famous mothers who run. The roster of champion mother-athletes is large, and it continues to grow. In Blankers-Koen's day, it was thought that maternity wore a woman out, that having a baby was a liability to a runner. No more.

W hat does one woman tell another in the changing room? Ingrid Kristiansen told the other great Norwegian mara-thoner Grete Waitz that having a baby had given her a real psychological boost: 'It helped give me other things to think about,'

Kristiansen said. 'It taught me there's another dimension to living.' Having a baby may also have improved her racing times.

Three months after her son Gaute was born, Ingrid Kristiansen sliced two minutes off her marathon time. Then she began to chop down world records, becoming the only athlete of either sex ever to hold the world 5,000 metres, 10,000 metres, and the marathon records at the same time. Then came the world best times in the half-marathon record, and at 15 kilometres.

Because gaunt, hollow-cheeked Ingrid Kristiansen was virtually all muscle, skin and bones, like many other top athletes (see the discussion of body weight in Chapter 6, Killer Gymnastics) she had temporarily stopped having periods. She didn't even realize she was pregnant until she was in her fifth month. She is one of many champions who have had a dramatic upsurge of ability after giving birth.[2] Kristiansen is the most impressive athlete of her era, as Fanny Blankers-Koen was of hers.

Now there is evidence that a champion will improve her personal best after she has a baby, provided she can keep up her training. Getting help with childcare is the major impediment to training. Star runners can afford to pay for backup help. Valerie Brisco, who was forty pounds overweight when her baby was born, got back into shape and won three gold medals at the 1984 Olympics. Two and a half years before the Games, Brisco had married former football player Alvin Hooks. Soon Alvin Jr. was accompanying her to workouts. Brisco was astonished at the effect motherhood seemed to be having: 'I know for a fact that it gave me extra strength. It's easier for me to work out well now.'

Sport scientists are still not quite sure why there is a post-natal peak in performance. There may be biological reasons. Kristiansen's coach has noticed that her gait has changed – a pelvis widened by childbirth may have contributed to a more efficient stride.

Because having a child is a formidable endurance event itself, mothers may gain an edge. Some scientists think that pregnancy makes women more resistant to pain and fatigue. And it gradually conditions the heart and lungs as it forces them to become more efficient to cope with extra bodyweight. For this reason, the British sports physiologist Craig Sharp calls pregnancy 'nature's own aerobic conditioner'.

Much of the benefit, however, in Kristiansen's case and in others, is psychological. Once an athlete has demonstrated that she is a

'When I began my comeback my second son was only one month old, and when I competed he was eight months old'

Dorothy Odam Tyler, 1936 and 1948 high jump silver medallist

'real woman', says the American sport psychologist Dorothy Harris, she is likely to have fewer conflicts about excelling in sport. What has happened, according to Harris's analysis, is that Kristiansen no longer feels her femininity is endangered by success.

Displacing the old worries that sport might imperil the female reproductive system is the evidence that having a baby can – for physiological and psychological reasons – enhance a woman champion's sport.

It is hard to know how many top athletes were pregnant when they competed at high level, or how pregnant they were. At the 1952 Helsinki Olympics, at least one bronze medalist was pregnant. The sprinter Evelyn Ashford had her daughter Raina in May, 1985, just forty weeks after breaking the world 100-metres record.

In 1948, when the *Daily Graphic* stressed the fact of Fanny Blankers-Koen's motherhood ('I shall train my two children to be athletes as well') it was to show she was a 'real woman', not a butch type. There were other mothers who achieved outstanding success at sport, but for nearly two decades no one noticed the pattern of improvement. The case of Irena Szewinska had made it hard to detect.

In a brilliant seventeen-year international athletic career, Szewinska, a Polish Jew (she had been Irena Kirzenstein until her marriage), won more major titles than had any other athlete in the history of track and field athletics. At three Olympics – in 1964, 1968 and 1976 – she won gold medals at track events. There were also two silver medals and two bronze medals.

Szewinska married her coach on Christmas Day, 1967. She took time off for her pregnancy and her son Andrzej was born in 1970. But she had trouble regaining her form. During this time she often came last in races. She was not really at peak fitness when she won the Olympic bronze medal at 200 metres in Munich in 1972.

Not till 1974 did she have another fine season, and it was an *annus mirabilis*. She defeated the remarkable East German runner Renate Stecher in the European Championships at 100 and at 200 metres, setting a new world 200-metres record of 23.2 seconds. No one had believed a woman would ever run under 50 seconds in the 400 metres. Szewinska, who had only run the distance for the first time in 1973, when she was already twenty-seven, did it. Then, at the 1976 Olympics, she bettered her own world 200-metres record by nearly half a second.

Eastern European sport scientists were the first to realize that

'The year away from the track did me good'

Irena Szewinska

'My mother and my husband care for my daughter when I have to run'

Runner Tatyana Kazankina, 1976 and 1980 Olympic champion

Mary Decker Slaney with son Ashley, 1987

mothers run best. A German sports scientist who was working in the United States seems to have written the first paper on the subject, but it was in the East, not the West, that notice was taken. But they had not yet learned to get it easily right in Szewinska's time. Whether she had sufficient child help and encouragement is not certain.

Now when Eastern-bloc athletes take a season off to have a baby – and increasingly they do – they quickly come back better than ever. In 1980, the tall East German sprinter Barbel Eckert Wockel, who took time out between Olympics to have a baby, became the first woman successfully to defend the 200-metres title. Her compatriot, the heptathlete Anke Vater Behmer, sat out the 1985 season to have a baby, and promptly won gold at the 1986 European Championships.

In the West, taking a season off for maternity began to catch on. After a glorious 1985 season on the track, Mary Decker Slaney sat out most of the next season, pregnant. Asked by a hostile *Times*man

Valerie Brisco-Hooks, the first athlete male or female to win both the 200 and 400 metres at a single Olympics, Los Angeles, 1984

if she had gotten pregnant because she thought it would improve her running, Slaney said that was one of the reasons. She saw no shame in it. Nor should she. Her post-natal comeback, however, has been hampered by injury, of which in her career, Decker Slaney has had more than her share.

It is important to note too that Szewinska, Decker Slaney and all the other women athletes who were having babies were at the age and in the circumstances of life when many women decide to have children. It was by no means simply to improve their sporting performance they were getting pregnant. But by the late 1970s, in sporting circles, it had become common knowledge that mothers run best.

As the 1988 track season opened, only two women were thought capable of breaking the next psychological barrier in the marathon, by running the distance faster than two hours twenty minutes, and neither of them had done it yet. One was Ingrid Kristiansen.

The other was Joan Benoit-Samuelsen (see Chapter 11, The Furthest Race). In Los Angeles in 1984, she had won the first ever Olympic marathon. At the time Joan Benoit (not yet Samuelsen) held the world record. It was bettered by Mama Ingrid Kristiansen.

Joan Benoit-Samuelsen didn't race marathons in 1987. She was pregnant. The baby, called Abigail, was born on 24 October. About two weeks later, a not yet fully recovered Benoit-Samuelsen finished an encouraging fifth in her first post-natal race, a little four-miler in Portland, Maine. By the Olympics she was expecting to be fighting fit.

CHAPTER 5

DEEP WATER

*D*awn Fraser smoked, drank, and had nearly as large a collection of ex-fiancés as she had swimsuits, and she had quite a few of those.[1] She liked to do what she liked to do. And she didn't see any reason to lie about it: 'I admit that I've done some damned silly things.'[2]

In the prim 1950s and what, in Australian swimming circles, were the equally prim 1960s, this did not go down well. Take 28 October 1962, the day she became the first woman ever to swim 100 metres in under a minute – it was the swimming equivalent of running the first ever four-minute mile. Officials chided Fraser, who was twenty-five, for revealing to newsmen that her celebration was going to be very alcoholic. 'I've grown up, and I don't see why I should be expected to pretend that I don't act like a grown-up,' she said.

Beer-drinking, though, was the least of it. From her first Olympic gold medal in 1956 to her forced retirement from competition eight years later, Dawn Fraser put the Australian swimming Establishment through a purgatory of pranks and problems.

They put her through hell.

She was their greatest champion. She ruled the glamour event of the pool, the 100-metres freestyle, also called the crawl, for an unheard-of dozen years. But despite her cache of Olympic gold, despite her thirty-nine world records, they almost wished she had been born somewhere else.

She wished they were dead.

Swimmers have been at loggerheads with swimming officials for generations. Nightclub singer Eleanor Holm came up against the stodginess of the American Olympic Committee on the transatlantic voyage to the Nazi Olympics. She held the world backstroke record, and was expected to retain her Olympic title in Berlin. She had knowingly ruined her blossoming, post-1932-Olympic Hollywood movie career by refusing to play swimming roles, even at $750 a week. Those roles would have made her a swimming professional and ineligible for the Olympics. Instead she sang with her husband's band.

On the liner SS *Manhattan*, Holm, a twenty-two-year-old 'sophisticated lady', was made to share a third-class stateroom with two very young swimmers. Possibly even they found the early-to-bed, early-to-rise, no-alcohol routine tedious. Eleanor Holm, who had been prevented from paying her own passage in first class, found it intolerable. She sneaked upstairs to drink champagne with the reporters, her favourite among them the actress Helen Hayes's ex-husband.

One night Eleanor Holm had too much champagne. She was discovered on her way back to her room. Her punishment, announced when they landed, was dismissal from the team. Ordered to go home immediately, she said she felt inclined to stay. The story made the front pages. Eleanor Holm was hired to report on the Games by the International News Service, and had a lively, no doubt memorable time, but the puritanical head of the Olympic Committee Avery Brundage saw to it that she never competed again.

The following year, Eleanor Holm became the star of the then famous Aquacade 'girlie revue', and before long could show off to visitors a flashy wardrobe of a hundred dresses, and two hundred and fifty bathing suits, including a rhinestone-studded number that cost $250.

Even before the Eleanor Holm brouhaha, another swimmer, Martha Norelius, had problems with stubborn authority. The bone of contention in the Eleanor Holm case had been morals. With Norelius, the issue was money.

Born in Stockholm, reared in the United States, Martha Norelius, whose father had swum for Sweden at the 1906 interim Games, became the Olympic 400-metre freestyle champion of 1924 and 1928. Those victories made her the first woman ever to retain a swimming title at successive Olympics. Besides that, she was the world's fastest woman over almost any distance for eight years. But in 1929 she was banned from amateur swimming for giving an

'I have my fun – and I think I'm a better swimmer because of it'

Dawn Fraser

'I still have my 1932 Olympic bathing suit'

Eleanor Holm, 1984

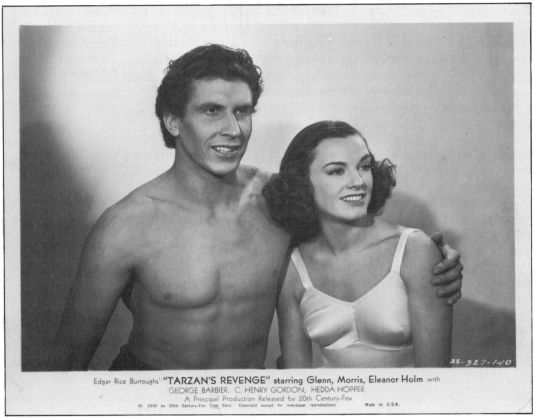

Edgar Rice Burroughs' "TARZAN'S REVENGE" starring Glenn, Morris, Eleanor Holm with
GEORGE BARBIER, C. HENRY GORDON, HEDDA HOPPER
A Principal Production Released by 20th Century-Fox
© 1937 by 20th Century-Fox Film Corp. Copyright waived for newspaper reproductions. Made in U.S.A.

exhibition swim in the same pool as professionals. She denied that she had herself received any money.

Fifty-two years later, in 1981, the English Olympic silver medallist Sharron Davies, another swimmer with a mind of her own, was put in her place through the rules on payments to amateurs, which even at that time, were more strictly enforced in swimming than in track and field and many other sports whose stars were gaining bankable reputations. Champions worldwide were now demanding the right to take control of their own lives. They wanted money and power. The swimming authorities were trying to still the upheaval that was shaking amateur sport.

Sharron Davies and her regular coach had distinct views on how she should train. However, the methods of the British team officials under whose jurisdiction Sharron Davies came just before major events were different. When Davies attempted to stick to methods

'They hurt me, but far worse is that they are damaging my sport; and for that I will never forgive them'

Sharron Davies

she knew worked, she was viewed as a troublemaker. They eventually got rid of her by pronouncing her a professional, banned from further competition, because she had received £40 for appearing on the television show *Give Us A Clue.* It was archaic (a woman has to live), and a very strict interpretation of the regulations.

The troubles that swimming officialdom had in bending Davies and her predecessors, Eleanor Holm and Martha Norelius, to their will were as nothing compared to what they faced with Dawn Fraser. The others were mavericks; she was a renegade. From Fraser's first Olympics, in Melbourne in 1956, to her reluctant retirement after the Tokyo Olympics in 1964, Dawn Fraser trained hard and played hard.

Officials everywhere prefer to deal with young swimmers, who are more likely to do as they are told. Young swimmers are by far the majority; most of the older ones tire of the rigours of training or are pushed out. Fraser was twenty-seven at her last Games, a dozen years older than her chief rival. By that time, even though there was an excellent chance that she might make a very special mark in Olympic history, Dawn Fraser and the Australian team officials were barely on speaking terms.

There were eight children in the Fraser family. Dawn, who was born on 4 September 1937, was the baby. She was coddled more than the baby of a family usually is, because she was so often ill. If there was a cold going around, little Dawnie got it, and as frequently as not it became bronchitis, once even pleurisy. Any such ailment was always complicated in Dawn's case with a scarey bout of bronchial asthma. During an asthma attack she was wheezy, coughed, and had such trouble breathing that she might have to sleep sitting up. At its worst, it felt as though there was a kangaroo sitting on her chest. The asthma was chronic and frequent and, as it turned out, not something she ever outgrew.

One of Dawn's four older brothers, Don, taught her to swim at a public pool when she was six. She used to dive from the high board on his back. The moist, warm air of the swimming pool was good for her asthma. After ten or twenty minutes in the swimming pool, she could feel her lungs open. She went often. She became one of a gang of kids, nearly all boys, who used to jump the turnstile at the public pool. 'We got as much satisfaction from those stolen swims as we did those days from the plums and apricots we'd steal from backyard gardens.'

The Fraser family lived in an old semi-detached house in Birchgrove Road, in a working-class suburb near the Sydney docks. Dawn's father insisted that all of his children learn a trade. Most of the boys would grow up to be carpenters. The girls, including Dawn, would learn dressmaking.

When she was eleven, one of Dawn Fraser's cousins, an amateur coach, enrolled her in a swimming club and began to work on her stroke. She was still eleven when she won her first club race, competing against grown women. 'It was the first thing I'd ever achieved in my life. Nobody had helped me get from the start to the finish and people were cheering and clapping when I climbed out of the water.' She was hooked on swimming.

In club races she was often pitted against boys and given half a second start because of her sex. 'I was beating them fairly regularly when I was twelve; but sometimes I'd be beaten, and I'd get furious with myself when that happened.

'I hated the easy assumption that girls *had* to be slower than boys.'

In 1951, her favourite brother Don died of leukaemia. Soon after, when she entered the Western Suburbs championships, her first amateur race, Dawn Fraser suffered another crushing blow, even though she narrowly won the race. She defeated the Sydney swimming prodigy Lorraine Crapp, who was an acknowledged world-champion-in-the-making. At the time, Lorraine Crapp seemed a more likely candidate to become Australian swimming's golden girl than did Dawn Fraser. Crapp was 'nicer', girlier, a more conventional and seemingly more reliable filler of the role. Crapp was a champion; this Fraser was an overaged upstart from the slums.

Lorraine Crapp was one year younger than Dawn Fraser, but she had started swimming earlier. She was small, blonde, with a rounded figure and a captivating smile. Fraser was bigger and far less delicate.

As a ranked swimmer, Lorraine Crapp had given Fraser a one-second start, in the Western championship, worth 18 inches to 2 feet in the pool over the 55-yard distance. Fraser won by less than that. Lorraine Crapp took the defeat well. But her coach Frank Guthrie saw Dawn Fraser as a threat he wanted to destroy. He asked her a lot of questions and she answered them, and he got madder and madder. 'By the time I went home to Balmain that day, I knew I was in trouble.'

'I hated the easy assumption that girls *had* to be slower than boys'

Dawn Fraser

65

To protect his interest, Guthrie complained to the authorities that fourteen-year-old novice swimmer Dawn Fraser was a professional, because her first swimming club, the one in which her cousin had enrolled her, and to which she no longer belonged, payed small cash prizes to swimmers who were sixteen and over. Because of the fuss Crapp's coach made, Dawn Fraser was banned as a professional. She would not be able to enter amateur competition again for eighteen months, and by that time, Lorraine Crapp's coach must have thought, a tough kid like Fraser would be working full time in a factory or pregnant.

The decision was unfair and stupid. It made Dawn Fraser wary of official pronouncements ever after. 'It was the first cruelty I ever had from swimming. I was heartbroken at first, but determined not to show it,' Dawn Fraser wrote in her autobiography, *Gold Medal Girl.* 'I couldn't believe that there were people who would want to keep me out of a sport I was growing to love. I felt puzzled and alone; it was a feeling I was going to experience quite a lot during my career.'

In 1952, things started looking up. Harry Gallagher, an exceptional coach who was versed in what would one day be called sports science, decided to take Dawn Fraser under his wing. He had watched her swimming at the local pool for over a year. He saw in her the proverbial rough diamond. It was he who had been Lorraine Crapp's first coach; he lost her when Frank Guthrie took her on for free. Now Gallagher felt he had encountered another raw talent.

Dawn Fraser had a good basic stroke and hated losing. To make her a champion he had to hone her technique, teach her to build her stamina and motivate her to train harder than any woman had trained before. And then he had to keep her training for what was likely to be years. Dawn Fraser was not the easiest kid to take under your wing. 'He was a strict disciplinarian; I hated all rules or regulations.' Eventually he persuaded her to let him teach her. Then, all he had to do was convince her parents.

Money, or rather the lack of it, almost ended Fraser's career right then and there. Her parents could not afford for any of their eight children to get private coaching of any sort. Gallagher's pool was further from home than the local public one. Because she would be away so much, Dawn would not be able to help her mother with chores. And why, they said, did she need lessons anyway, she already knew how to swim?

Harry Gallagher said she had something special, the makings of a champion. But the recipe had to be right. He took her on as his first unpaid pupil on the condition that she did what he told her. She would have to bicycle ten miles a day back and forth for swimming lessons. His first instruction was to get a light for the bicycle.

On her first day at Gallagher's pool, Dawn Fraser, tough teenager, discovered she was to train with a flock of well-mannered eight- and nine-year-olds who were used to swimming a mile or a mile and a half every day before school. The amazing thing is that recalcitrant Fraser stuck it out.

Those children, Fraser and a few other swimmers were the vanguard of the revolution that was then going on in Australian swimming. Harry Gallagher and a few other top coaches – including the man he liked least, Frank Guthrie – were working with Professor Frank Cotton, a physiologist who probably knew as much as anyone in the world about what made athletes tick. Many of their swimmers were taken to Sydney University for heart, lung and blood tests. Athletes in other sports were tested too. These coaches had noticed that in recent years the only Australians who won medals had trained in the United States, where conditioning was taken very seriously. Now Australian officials and coaches began to use Professor Cotton's sports science to learn the most efficient way of conditioning a swimmer.

Dawn Fraser was the right woman in the right place.

In the summer of 1953, racing for New South Wales at the State championship, she took part in her first sanctioned amateur races since the ban. She finished third in the 110-yard sprint; Lorraine Crapp won it. But Crapp did not enter the 220, and Fraser won.

That got Dawn Fraser her first berth at the Australian national championships, in Melbourne in February 1954, where she finished an unexceptional third over 110 yards. On a night when there was no racing, Fraser went out with a boy on the Tasmanian team until 11 pm, when the other swimmers were long asleep. She had not asked permission to go, although permission was clearly required by team rules. It was her first infringement. She got off with a warning. As she continued to break rules, officials would become less understanding.

Two problems, the clashes with officialdom and lack of money, would plague Dawn Fraser throughout her career. Being coached by Harry Gallagher, however, was to be almost entirely unproblematic. He was keeping her on, at no charge, for as long as it took.

At seventeen, Fraser had temporarily become a squeaky-clean athlete, who got up at five in the morning to put on the family's breakfast porridge before bicycling off to Drummonyne Baths. Aside from the enlightened coaching, the secret of her training was her training partner, Gallagher's other star pupil, Jon Henricks. 'He was always out front, setting the pace.' She had to swim hard to keep up. Thereafter she always tried to train with boys and men. 'I've always wanted the best of the boys ahead of me, making it hard.' It may have been accidental, Henricks and her swimming together for the first times; it was not a commonplace idea for female champions in any sport to train with men – although it is now.

In 1955, she won her first national title. In July of that year, Gallagher got a better job in a pool in Adelaide, more than a thousand miles away as the crow flies. He went to see her parents again because he wanted to take their daughter with him. She would live at the pool, chaperoned by his parents; and they would help her find a job. Her parents agreed seventeen-year-old Dawn could try it for six months.

In Adelaide, the first thing she did every day was swim; the last thing she did was swim again. She had started with Gallagher at about a mile a day (which sometimes she unofficially cut short). Now she was swimming eight miles a day. Besides that she used the gymnasium at the pool, watched training films and videos of her own performances.

Like every swimmer there, she was monitored by videos and laboratory tests, which were used to set training loads and to adapt diet. The swimmers were given large doses of vitamins. Fraser took a hundred tablets a week, which she says were vitamins A, B1, B2, C and D, and iron. With so many Australian swimmers downing huge quantities of tablets, there began to be rumours that they were taking some secret wonder drug. Anabolic steroids and other drugs would not be tested for or banned from the Olympics until 1968.

There was a laboratory assistant too who ran experiments on rats to test diet theories. Gallagher's findings were co-ordinated with a dietician, a heart specialist, a physiotherapist and a radiologist. This was sports training of a very modern sort. It would soon be practised worldwide.

In February 1956, at the national championships, Dawn Fraser put in a 100-metre superswim of 64.5 seconds, which was not only good enough for victory and a new world record, but it broke the longest-standing world swimming record there was, which had

'I've been trying for years to swim just one perfect race'

Dawn Fraser

stood for twenty years. If that were not joy enough, in the race Fraser defeated Lorraine Crapp. That same week, Dawn Fraser broke the world 220-yard and 200-metres records. She was sticking to the swimming sprints; because of her asthma, she felt she didn't have the breath for longer races.

As the 1956 Melbourne Olympics approached, Australia went sports crazy. The Games had never been held in Australia before. Australian sport flourished. On the tennis courts Hoad, Laver, Rosewall and others won; on the racing track, Jack Brabham became world champion. When tickets to the Olympics went on sale, the runner Betty Cuthbert, who was eighteen, bought some for track and field events because she never dreamed she would make the athletics team. Dawn Fraser, who was now nineteen, was more confident. She even believed she might win a medal.

At the Games, Betty Cuthbert, who came from Merrylands near Sydney, ran to victory in the 100 metres, 200 metres, and 4 × 100 metres relay. She had not even been ranked in the world's top fifteen in 1955.

Ten days before Dawn Fraser's first event, she was admitted to the Olympic Village hospital. 'I had an earache, an eye infection, bad headaches; and I had to have penicillin injections every day for a week.' Those were a lot of symptoms for just one swimmer. Some of them were thought to be psychosomatic. But the penicillin seemed to do the trick.

The night before her first Olympic final, Dawn Fraser had a nightmare. Her feet were stuck to the starting blocks with honey. When at last, she dived into the swimming pool, she realized it was filled with spaghetti instead of water. She landed in a tangle of spaghetti. She couldn't get out. It was in her mouth. She couldn't breathe. She woke up trembling and in need of her asthma adrenalin spray.

At the pool before the race Gallagher, feeling good because Jon Henricks had won the men's 100-metres freestyle, greeted her with, 'How do you feel, champ?'

'I feel as if I'm waiting for an execution,' she told him. 'My own execution.'

'You'll kill 'em,' he said.

Fraser had bought tickets to the Olympics for her parents. They were sitting in the huge crowd waiting for the race. The eight tense swimmers marched out to the edge of the 50-metre pool. Dawn Fraser knew that Lorraine Crapp was the one it would be toughest to beat. At the first whistle, the swimmers stripped off their warm-ups. At the second whistle, they stood behind their blocks. At a third whistle, they mounted their blocks. Dawn Fraser's stomach felt queasy. She took a few deep breaths, and stood coiled, knees bent, ready to go. The starter's pistol sounded.

She hit the water like a torpedo and didn't take a breath until she had gone fifteen metres. Gallagher's careful race plan, her tactics, were forgotten; everything she did was instinctive. Fraser led into the first turn, but Crapp came out of her turn ahead. Twenty-five metres from the finish they were level, but Fraser felt she had gone too fast too early. Over the last ten metres she could feel herself flagging. They touched the edge of the pool together; it wasn't immediately clear which of them had won. They waited together in the pool. 'Then an official winked at me and held up one finger. I'd made it. I was the champion of the world.'

She had won the 100-metres freestyle in a new world record time of 62.0 seconds. In the 400 metres, Dawn Fraser got silver behind Lorraine Crapp. The two then joined forces with two other swimmers to win the 4 × 100 metres relay in world record time.

The Australian swimmers did so well that rumours of pep pills and other drugs were revived. After the Games, there was a story that a cleaner had found some half-eaten oranges which had an odd odour. They were in the American team's changing room. According to the story, never verified, the oranges had been injected with some sort of dope. The use of white and black magic in sport science – legitimate monitoring, and cheating with dope – was now an issue in Olympic sport.

The issue of money was still there. Now that she was an Olympic champion, the swimming Establishment kept a watchful eye on whether or not Fraser was earning any money from the sport, that being utterly against the rules. Even her job as a trainee fashion buyer at a big store was suspect for a while – if they could have proved that she got it by dint of being a swimmer, they would have declared her a professional again.

She was, though, forced to give up a scholarship to the University of Texas, her one chance of a university education, because the Australian officials said she would lose her place on the team that went to the Commonwealth Games and other top competitions if she went to Texas even for a year. She might be able to gain a place for the Olympics anyway, they said, if she flew home for the trials, at her own expense. But that, they knew, was much too expensive.

What she wanted most was to swim for Australia. So, she says, 'I kept on selling sportswear in Adelaide.'

Rome, 1960. Pope John XXIII blessed the visiting athletes and organizers. The next day church bells tolled the opening of the Games. At the Stadio del Nuoto, the Australians and the Americans split the swimming medals. Of fifteen events, they missed just one title. It went to Anita Lonsbrough, the tall, broad-shouldered, nineteen-year-old from Yorkshire, England, who won the 200-metres breaststroke in a world record time of 2 minutes 49.5 seconds, having cut back a four-foot deficit during the race. Before the race, when the other swimmers were visibly jittery, Anita Lonsbrough had sat calmly beside the pool polishing her nails.

An exuberant Dawn Fraser retained her 100-metres title. She became the first woman ever to win that swimming title at the Olympics twice in a row.

But there had been a lot of unhappiness in the Australian camp. Lorraine Crapp, who was twenty-two, had evoked a bitter storm. By now, Dawn Fraser and Lorraine Crapp were friends if not bosom buddies. Each specialized in a different event. Crapp had been the first woman to swim 400 metres in five minutes, and she was expected to retain her Olympic 400-metre freestyle title. Crapp had secretly gotten married on the eve of the Games.

For as long as they could, Fraser and a few other swimmers covered for her when she sneaked out at night to stay with her husband while they were in Rome – it was not against Olympic rules, but Lorraine Crapp was afraid she would be stopped by the Australian authorities. She was. Her Games were ruined.

Fraser was disgusted and said so, especially since the Australian runner Herb Elliot, whose wife had accompanied him to Rome, was allowed by track officials to see her. And permission had been given to the swimmer Murray Rose to sleep away from the Olympic Village, in the apartment where his parents were staying.

Now Fraser found herself in conflict with the Australian authorities ostensibly over the butterfly race. Well before the Olympics, she had collapsed with terrible stomach cramps during butterfly training. She had been the world record holder in the butterfly, but she gave up the stroke. She says a doctor told her to. Her coach was told; it is possible the swimming authorities were not, possible too that they didn't care what she wanted as they were in charge.

After her great Olympic victory, per usual, Fraser partied hard till late in the night. As she understood it (she says she asked), she was to have a free day. She spent the morning exploring the streets of Rome on foot. At about two o'clock that afternoon, shortly after she had finished a large plate of pasta, she was told abruptly that she was to swim in an hour, in the butterfly lap of the medley relay heats.

Fraser refused to swim, saying she would be no good because of the morning's walking and the food, and anyway she didn't want to do the butterfly.

You don't refuse to swim. She knew there was going to be trouble. She was made to feel an outcast for the duration of the Games, and after the Games the Australian officials showed their displeasure by leaving their star out of the swimming tours of Japan and South Africa. They knew she liked to travel.

Her response was to swim better than ever before. No woman had ever swum 100 metres in a minute. Her dream was to be the first to do it, thereby breaking the biggest psychological and physical barrier of sprint swimming.

On 23 October 1962, she clocked exactly a minute. Four days later, she cut a tenth of a second from the time. She sliced the record by milli-seconds twice more, the last time to 58.9 seconds on 29 February 1964. That record stood until 1972. In all, she held the record for the 100-metres freestyle for sixteen years (1956–1972). 'The strange thing about that one minute barrier was that once I proved to myself that I could get inside it, it stopped being any sort of barrier for me.'

Now Dawn Fraser had another ambition. No swimmer had ever won the 100-metres sprint title three times in a row – in fact, no swimmer had ever held any Olympic title three times in succession. Her new aim was to do exactly that in Tokyo. She had no doubt that she would be reinstated on the team: 'When there were gold medals to be won, it seemed that there was no doubt of any kind about my worthiness to represent Australia.'

But something terrible happened in March of the Olympic year. She was driving with her mother, her sister and a friend, and crashed into a parked truck. Her mother was killed, her sister and friend required surgery. Fraser herself had a chipped neck vertebra and severe shock. Immobilized, she lay in bed thinking her own depressed thoughts.

There were five hundred letters of sympathy, and two and a half

The first ever Olympic swimming dead-heat: Carrie Steinseifer and Nancy Hogshead tied for gold in the 100 metres freestyle, Los Angeles. *Below:* Anke Mohring setting the world 10,000 metres record, Strasbourg 1987. *Opposite:* Sharron Davies

thousand cards – including one from the swimmer who had become Tarzan in the movies, Johnny Weissmuller, and many from swimmers around the world, cabinet ministers and sporting organizations. But there was no word of condolence, she says, from the Australian Swimming Union.

It seemed to her that they almost wished they had got rid of her too – despite the fact that she was the most outstanding swimmer Australia had ever had.

Somehow, she found the mental strength to resume training her battered body with the intensity that was required for the Olympics, which were only seven months away.

Tokyo, 1964. For the first time the Games were being staged in Asia. Many Westerners arrived expecting kimonos, kabuki dancers, exoticism, but few of the conveniences of Western life. They were stunned by what they saw. At the opening ceremony, jet planes hurled five interlocking Olympic rings into the sky. Japan was now a great economic world power. The years of being a source of shoddy goods were over. To those who hadn't noticed, the Olympics made that plain. The Olympic stadium and pool and the Olympic Village were large, modern, efficient, expensive and new.

Dawn Fraser nearly missed that impressive opening ceremony. Because her first race was within three days of the opening of the Games, she was forbidden to march in the ceremony which went on for hours. She had missed the ceremony in Rome for the same reason, and this time she rebelled. She and some other swimmers sneaked into the ceremony anyway. She saw Yoshinori Sakai, born in Hiroshima the day the atom bomb fell, carry the Olympic flame into the stadium. She saw the flags of ninety-four nations, and marched with most of the 5,140 competitors, 683 of them women, in procession.

Once again the Australian officials were angry. They treated her like a very naughty little girl, despite the fact that at twenty-seven she was now the senior citizen of world swimming. Lorraine Crapp's career was long over. The swimming world was full of 'water babies' now.

Just before the Olympics, Fraser had gone down with a virus infection. It had led to a bout of the asthma she had had since childhood. Tension, which makes one's chest tight, aggravates asthma. On the eve of the 100-metres freestyle race, she was suffering from a cold complicated by asthma. She was wheezy and short of breath. There seemed to be no chance of making Olympic history by winning her event for the third time in a row.

About an hour before the race, the doctor said he didn't like the sound of her chest. He gave her some tablets, and suggested she think about pulling out of the race. Fraser wouldn't hear of it.

Fifty minutes later, she took a couple of puffs of her counter-asthma spray. Asthma medicines were and are legal. Then she went to the pool. The gun sounded, she dived, and began swimming for the Olympic title. She led the first lap by half a body length. Because of her breathing difficulties, she dare not do the usual fast tumble turn. Instead, she settled for an open swivel turn on the surface. It was slower. Sharon Stouder, the fifteen-year-old Californian every-one had been hearing about, was swimming well. Now the crowd yelled as the two swam for all they were worth in a stroke-for-stroke battle down the length of the pool. It would be Stouder's first medal, and probably Fraser's last. Seconds from the end of the race, Fraser sprinted forward, winning in 59.5 seconds, a new Olympic record, and .4 seconds ahead of young Stouder.

To celebrate her victory, Dawn Fraser and two men she knew sneaked into the gardens of the Imperial Palace, climbed up a flagpole and 'souvenired' a flag. They were suddenly surrounded by police and taken to a Tokyo police station. The charges were dropped when the police realized she was Dawn Fraser, and the Emperor made her a gift of the flag.

The Australian officials were not so forgiving. She was banned from swimming for ten years, the intention clearly being to end her career. That ruling was followed by the announcement that she had won an MBE, one of Australia's highest honours. It was not awarded by the Swimming Union.

Four years later she was reinstated as an amateur, but it was much too late to get into racing shape for the 1968 Olympics. She went to the Games anyway, as a guest of the Mexican organizing committee, and saw her title go to Jan Henne, an American, in a slow time, 60 seconds flat. But for the rigidity of the swimming officialdom, it is conceivable that she would have won that title a fourth time.

Her record of three consecutive wins in the same swimming event has never been beaten.

'Nobody had helped me get from the start to the finish and people were cheering and clapping when I climbed out of the water'

Dawn Fraser

CHAPTER 6

KILLER GYMNASTICS

Munich, 1972. The smallest gymnast on the team, carrying the huge team bag on her shoulder, is the last one in the line when the Soviet team walks in graceful procession into the Olympic Sporthalle. This is the team which has won the Olympic title five times in a row. They are all fine gymnasts. But the little one, whom that enormous bag is almost obscuring from view, the little one who only just made the team as a reserve, is about to create a sensation.

The newcomer, Olga Korbut, looks about eleven or twelve. She is virtually straight up and down, a pretty child. On her delicately-boned, four-foot eleven-inch, 84-pound body there is little fat and no sign of puberty. The first surprise of her Olympic gymnastics debut was that Olga Korbut was fully seventeen.

The Soviet team was known for its aloof perfection. This Olga Korbut was an able gymnast too, but she was different. She flirted with the audience, winked, tossed that blonde head, strutted. She looked like an innocent child. She behaved like Lolita. Standing in for a member of the team who was ill, Korbut performed in the team competition. She charmed the audience with her gymnastics as well as with her coquettish ways, earning high scores – the lowest a more-than-respectable 9.4 out of 10.0 – and qualifying for the second stage of the competition, which featured the thirty-six gymnasts who had performed best in the team competition.

Only two other gymnasts had more points to carry over to the next stage than Olga Korbut with 38.350. She now had a good chance of winning the most sought-after of all gymnastics titles: the all-round, or overall, championship. Her strength was in the optional routines. Hers were imaginative and daring, even danger-ous. The reason Olga Korbut was on the team only as a reserve was

Olga Korbut, the star of Munich

79

that despite her ability to do some marvellous, complicated routines, sometimes she muffed the simple compulsory exercises. But things this first day were going well.

Then, suddenly, she made two mistakes during her thirty seconds on the uneven parallel bars. Her feet touched the floor. They weren't supposed to. Her hand momentarily slipped off the bar. Practically beginner's errors. She continued her performance anyway, as gymnasts are taught to do, to the end, but scored only 7.5. Those mundane errors had lost her the chance of an overall medal.

'It is my character to win'

Olga Korbut

Unable to hide her disappointment, at the end of her performance Olga Korbut wept. Satellite television was watching. An audience of four hundred million saw her cover her face with her hands and cry. It was a touching sight. Hers would become the most famous tears in sport.

The timing was right. A girl who could be graceful and cry, who was a champion without visible muscles, was to many people a welcome sight. It came at a time when in Western countries, many parents had begun to worry that their daughters might want to play football or run the marathon. The idea of women's liberation was taking hold, and even spreading to sport. Billie Jean King was in the news. She and some of the other tennis players had become fed up with the raw deal they were getting compared to male players, and had started their own women's professional circuit, which was thriving. Girls were asking why they couldn't join teams in what had always been boys' sports. The women who competed at the Olympics had attained so high a standard in so many sports that sex tests had been instituted at the previous Games to make sure they were not men in disguise.

A revolution was bubbling up in women's sport. But when Olga Korbut went all girlie on the television screen, there were plenty of people out there not only eager to comfort her, but willing to embrace her as a way of holding back the tide of change – if only she could be a winner.

The next day was like a Hollywood movie. With the audience rooting for her, everything began to go right. She did a half back somersault on the uneven bars which no one else had ever done. The crowd and the judges gasped. It was a difficult, dangerous, innovative manoeuvre. It had taken Olga Korbut, whose short body it was designed specially for, fully two years to learn to do it. She must have practised it twenty thousand times.

The backward somersault she did on the long, four-inch-wide plank called the beam had never been done before either. The judges were anxious: should such perilous innovations be rewarded or banned?

The crowd was exhilarated. They cheered her every move, and Korbut held on to her concentration. Early on, when the judges' marks were low, the crowd in the Sporthalle booed and stomped. At one point, the jeering went on for five tense minutes. In the next event, there were signs that the judges had been affected.

On the balance beam, Korbut was awarded a generous 9.90. Purists said the judges were overmarking her, pandering to the partisan crowd. There were accusations that they overmarked in the floor exercise too.

With those two golds and her share of the Soviet team gold medal, plus one silver medal on the uneven bars, Olga Korbut came fifth overall. The most coveted Olympic title in the sport, the individual overall championship, went to another, more flawless Soviet gymnast, Ludmila Tourischeva, but it was Korbut who had become a star.

Girls by the millions took up gymnastics after Olga Korbut's Olympic debut. They and their parents did not realize that Korbut had made her sport dangerous. They only knew she had excelled at a sport where girls could be girls. No muscles needed – or so it appeared – just grace.

In fact, that was a lie. Strength is as important a factor as skill. Korbut had trained rigorously in a special gymnastics school since the age of ten to build the required muscle.

At her school near Minsk in Grodno, Russia, there were five hundred girls, but only she had learned to do those special somersaults. Her coach Renald Knysh had designed both of Olga Korbut's difficult new moves specifically to suit her body. He had designed them to be dangerous and difficult and to look it – to impress the judges.

Not everyone liked Renald Knysh, a dark-haired man who didn't talk much, and who disliked noise, even applause. But few doubted his devotion to his profession. He kept a cardfile of young married couples in the town who might bear children whom he might train in gymnastics. He worked his gymnasts hard. There were people who said he would stop at nothing to produce champions.

There were rumours that he had staved off Olga Korbut's puberty with drugs. Only a short-waisted, childlike body was flexible

'Olga Korbut was always smiling and real peppy'
Mary Lou Retton, 1984 Olympic champion

enough to do some of the routines Korbut was introducing into the sport. Only that sort of body, unburdened by fatty tissue like breasts, had the right strength-to-weight ratio. The womanly classical gymnasts of old would never have been able to do what Korbut did.

Not only the judges were impressed with what Olga Korbut could do. So were young gymnasts. Korbut and Knysh's new Killer Gymnastics changed the face of the sport. The Korbut somersault and the Korbut loop, once considered daring, still considered dangerous, have virtually became necessary for anyone who wants to win. Ever after, 'girlish' gymnastics would require enormous courage.

Montreal, 1976. Olga Korbut had invented Killer Gymnastics. Now Nadia Comaneci perfected it. With exquisite technique, she won three gold medals and a bronze. She was only fourteen at the time, stood Korbut's height – four foot eleven – but weighed 86 pounds, two pounds more. She was the first gymnast to score a perfect score of 10.0 at the Olympics. They called her Little Miss Perfect.

The distinguished Romanian coach Bela Karolyi had discovered her when she was only six. He was scouting for talent and saw her, in Onesti, Romania, in the schoolyard during recess. He liked the way she moved. As he was going over to talk to her, the schoolbell rang and the children ran into their classrooms.

Karolyi went into every classroom to find her. But how could he tell, the children were sitting down? Finally, he asked each class if they liked gymnastics. Nadia Comaneci was one of the ones who shouted, 'I do.' Until then she was an ordinary dark-haired child. Her father was a car mechanic; her mother an office worker. She had a younger brother called Adrian.

Now Karolyi saw to it she had fine training, and took the sport seriously. At the early age of seven Comaneci was entered in the Romanian junior championships; she finished thirteenth. At eight, she won. She was a student at the special gymnastics high school in Gheorghiu Dej. At just thirteen, she won the women's European championship, one of the hardest of all competitions because the Eastern European nations, who for years have dominated the sport, compete there. In 1976, with two coaches, a choreographer, a physician, an assistant music master, and a masseur to assist her, Nadia Comaneci became, at fourteen years 313 days old, the youngest ever Olympic gold medallist in the sport.

'I was gifted, that's all'

Nadia Comaneci

Comaneci made the sport riskier by adding a full turn to her dismount routine. 'The world has me to thank or blame for the Comaneci Somersault and the Comaneci Dismount,'[1] she says. On the blind forward somersault done on the high bar, 'the gymnast doesn't get to see the bar while trying to catch it until the last possible moment.'

In this new Killer Gymnastics, grace was not as necessary as courage. To win, you had to pick up 'bonus points' for risk. The injury level began to go up in the sport. Bones and joints were subjected to impact and squashed and stretched – they were stressed – over and over and over, thousands of times. This was damaging growing bones and joints, possibly stunting growth.[2]

But Nadia Comaneci also had another problem. She began to grow up. To save her career, when at sixteen her breasts budded and she grew taller, Comaneci instinctively stopped eating. She became the first famous anorexic gymnast. The need to stay skinny and childlike – pre-pubescent – has resulted in gymnastics having the highest percentage of anorexia of any sport. Coaches call it the Nadia Syndrome.

Anorexia is not, literally, contagious. But many young gymnasts modelled their behaviour on Comaneci. Two top British champions came down with anorexia. Nearly half of the gymnasts in a key California study[3] were eating less than two-thirds of the recommended daily allowances of vitamin B6, iron, calcium and zinc, all essential for normal growth. More than three-quarters of the college-age gymnasts studied in Michigan in 1986 had some sort of eating disorder associated with trying to stay thin.[4]

In Texas, at the 1979 world championships, Nadia Comaneci showed all the signs of anorexia – among them weakness, pallor, low resistance to infection and injury, wounds that would not heal. Although she was really too ill to perform, Comaneci was told to make an appearance to save the team's chances. She went on, but she made a mistake on a simple move.

Then she was taken to a nearby hospital with an inflamed wound on her wrist which had not healed. The greatest danger to a gymnast of being anorexic is that it makes her weak, prone to injury.

Moscow, 1980. Gymnastics practice, three days before the Olympic Games. Elena Mukhina, aged twenty, the daring world overall champion is practising for the Games. Elena Mukhina has already contributed something new to her sport: she has added a full twist to Korbut's high bar loop, catching the high bar once again and continuing with her routine. This new move, which took two years to learn, has increased the risk of the sport, but it is enthralling to watch. Mukhina must practise every aspect of her performance.

Now, as she practises the floor exercise, probably the least dangerous part of a gymnast's performance, she makes a mistake. In the final somersault of her tumbling sequence there is a standard gymnastics movement called a one and a half or one and three-quarter Arabian front somersault. She has to land on her neck and shoulders and then roll to a standing position. Mukhina has practised the Arabian over and over, probably well over 10,000 times. This time, she lands on her neck too heavily. It breaks.

She is hurried to a well-equipped hospital, she undergoes surgery, her life is saved. But Elena Mukhina is now paralysed from the neck down. For six months she cannot even talk. How could this happen to a world champion?

In her tribute to Mukhina, Nadia Comaneci said, 'As one of the world's top gymnasts, she could be expected to include many elements of high risk, in order to give her a chance of acquiring the necessary bonus points.'[5] In other words, the higher in the scale you got, the more perilous the sport was. Elena Mukhina, who had enthralled world audiences, was, Comaneci said in conclusion and intending no bitter irony, 'a fine exponent of our sport'.

After the accident, she never walked again. After arduous physiotherapy, much of it painful, which she undertakes with the same intensity as she did her championship moves, Mukhina can now sit up in a special chair. She believes that one day she will be able to walk.

In 1986 Olga Korbut, long retired, proposed an alternative to Killer Gymnastics. Why not, she said, have age categories at Olympic level? Then, girls who had become women could stay in competition. Physically, anorexia would no longer be such an occupational hazard.

We might even see a return of the grace of the classical gymnasts, the grown-ups like the great Czech Olympic champion Vera Caslavska. The pre-pubescent grouping, with its elastic contortions would have its audience; the ballerinas would have theirs. Korbut's ideas are theoretically viable. Unfortunately, it isn't likely anyone will up and change the sport soon, if ever.

No one knows how much of the postponement of puberty is done

> **'Gymnastics does put a young girl at risk – it can cause damage to a developing body'**
>
> **Nadia Comaneci**

individually by gymnasts who become anorexic, and how much is inflicted by coaches and sports doctors. In fact, you might say it is all inflicted because what the anorexic is responding to is her coach's message, the audience's message, to stay a child so she can do those Killer Gymnastics contortions.

The Soviets seem to be the first to have discovered that it may be possible to hold off puberty without drugs. Usually, just making sure a young gymnast's body fat is below seven per cent of body weight is enough. Some estimates say it can even be a bit higher. Most competitive gymnasts fall in the eight to nine per cent range. The body weight of most teenaged girls is about twenty per cent fat. Like marathoners, champion gymnasts are particularly thin. Even Lisa Elliott, the British national gymnastics champion, who is nowhere near the top of the world, has only 5.3 per cent body fat. This is close to the level of the Soviet stars.

It is possible that some gymnasts worldwide now use drugs, to delay puberty, or to stunt growth, and to build muscle power. There is no proof, though, and everyone denies it. It may just be that short girls in the West are attracted to the sport, and are sought out in the Eastern bloc.

Before and after Lolita: Vera Caslavska (*opposite*) won in Mexico in 1968; Mary Lou Retton (*left*) in Los Angeles in 1984

The 1984 overall Olympic champion Mary Lou Retton, a four-foot nine-inches tall American from the hills of West Virginia, is the first American ever to win an Olympic gymnastics title. She is the first to credit her coach, Bela Karolyi, the Romanian who discovered Nadia Comaneci, but now lives in the United States. Retton tells fond tales of his slave-driving. But so eager was she to train, that she didn't have to be prodded to remove the cast on her fractured wrist early and against doctor's orders. Retton won the Olympic title at the age of sixteen but has the aches and pains of a sixty-year-old. 'When it's cold and damp outside', she says, 'I just ache all over.'

The 1987 world champion, Aurelia Dobre, who won the title at the age of fifteen, is a superb technician, in the Romanian tradition of gymnastics perfection. She looks pert and small, childlike, a typical Killer Gymnast.

Her predecessor as world champion, Oksana Omelianchik, tiny and two years older, has made innovations in the floor exercise that are breathtaking and a little scarey. Her immediate change of direction after her first tumbling pass steps up the pace of floor exercise. Omelianchik, who trains in Kiev, brushes aside talk of anorexia or special diets or drugs. So does her coach and the head of the Soviet team. Long hours of training, they say, are the only secret of gymnastics.

CHAPTER 7

HORSE SENSE

*T*here were two distinct *dis*advantages to being a princess.
There were also many advantages. Princess Anne Elizabeth
Alice Louise was given her first pony, a small, shaggy Shetland
called William, when she was just two and a half. As soon as she
outgrew him, another pony appeared: Greensleeves, followed by
Mayflower, Bandit, and then 14.2-hand High Jinks, who was
stabled near her boarding school. There was also the advantage of
having access to and money for the very finest riding instruction.
There was, most important of all, the self-confidence, the carefully
nurtured sense of oneself, that a princess, like a champion, has to
have.

The stables of her mother Queen Elizabeth II were famous. The
Queen herself was and is a very competent horsewoman. She still
rides four or five times a week, and is an expert on horsebreeding.
To whom would bloodlines appeal, if not to a queen? The Queen's
husband, the Duke of Edinburgh, was quite a decent polo player;
their son Prince Charles soon took to the sport too. Polo isn't
regarded as a girls' game, although in distant ages, it was played by
Persian women. Polo is in fact less arduous and no more dangerous
than three-day eventing, which was to become the Princess's
sport.

'I'd have been quite happy (if I had been given the chance) to have
had a shot at playing polo,' Princess Anne says. 'I'd watched it since
the year dot and always enjoyed it.'[1] The year dot must have been
very soon after her birth on 15 August 1950.

Because theirs was a particularly horsey family – even the post
was brought by coach – it was natural, she says, to immerse herself
in some form of equestrian sport. 'Horses were always around. So,

in logical terms it would have been daft to have gone off and started archery.'

You need good horses – no, excellent horses – in three-day eventing. Not all expensive horses are excellent; but very nearly all excellent horses are expensive. This is true even though it takes years of instruction, practice and very hard work to turn a horse (and a rider) into a three-day eventer of Olympic standard.

'I'd have been quite happy to have had a shot at playing polo'

Princess Anne

This is where the first disadvantage of being a princess came in. Although Princess Anne's mother is one of the richest women in the world, she and her husband Philip are known to be a little stingy when it comes to paying out for horseflesh. 'There is one trait, almost a failing, in the Royal Family,' says the necessarily diplomatic royal biographer Nicholas Courtney, 'and that is that they do not spend enough money on their horses . . . The Queen's bloodlines at her stud are no longer top-flight, and this is reflected in her declining [racing] success on the flat.'

Like mother, like son, or so it seemed when Prince Charles bought the wrong horse to begin on in steeplechasing. He had refused a better one because it was too expensive. The Prince of Wales is thrifty when it comes to polo ponies too, often picking up rejects from the Royal stud. His father, the Duke of Edinburgh, doesn't like to see waste either. His daughter Anne's first serious eventing horse was one of his polo ponies that had shot up to 16.2 hands, too big for polo. The horse's name was Doublet.

As it turned out, Princess Anne was lucky in Doublet, although he certainly was not an easy ride. 'He was undoubtedly the quickest stopper I'd ever come across,' she says. 'I disappeared over his head so frequently that people used to say to Alison: Why is she riding that dangerous horse when she keeps falling off it?'

Alison Oliver, a former competitor and a top instructor, was then Princess Anne's riding instructor. She would have noticed, as did the Princess's previous instructor, that Anne had the courage and the desire to ride any horse or pony in sight – if she was allowed to.

Like Princess Anne's two novice eventing horses, Purple Star and Royal Ocean, Doublet had been sent for training up to Oliver. Oliver was working hard on the horse – and on the rider. Anne was born a princess; she had to learn to be a champion horsewoman.

Which brings us to the second disadvantage of being a princess. Not many novice riders have to put up with gossip columnists and newspaper photographers watching their every fall. Princess Anne did. Who dares wins, the saying goes. Who dares often falls off a horse too.

'When I'm approaching a water jump with dozens of photographers waiting for me to fall in, and hundreds of spectators wondering what's going to happen next, the horse is just about the only one who doesn't know I'm Royal.'

Being in the public eye may have made Princess Anne more cautious than she was innately. And even if it didn't, it was a psychological burden, an extra weight she and Doublet had to carry. There were in fact two disconcerting sides to the public interest in her: every failure was photographed and appeared in the national press; and any success – such as elevation to the Olympic team – might be ascribed to her being a princess rather than to her skill as a horsewoman.

Three-day eventing is a sport of thrills and spills. It begins quietly enough with the graceful rigours of the dressage test, a set series of movements, for which the horse has to be calm and obedient and well-taught. It ends with a civilized bout of showjumping. But midway, in the cross-country competition, the sport becomes wild and woolly.

Riding cross-country on open terrain, with its (sometimes specially constructed) sudden hills and concavities, horse and rider must jump over thirty or more cunningly-devised, often complicated fences. They are erected at awkward distances and at testing angles. Riders are allowed to walk the course (without the horses) the day before the competition, but on the day there are often unhappy surprises. The weather may change, transforming soft ground into a quagmire. Even slight changes in the contour, perhaps caused by another rider's mishap, may force one to take a fence in a way different than planned, and then one may find that one is not safe at all, but sorry.

Three-day eventing was originally regarded as a test of officers and later also of non-military gentlemen. It was devised to make certain that officers' chargers were fighting fit. An all-round test of horse and rider, it is the most demanding and spectacular of all equestrian sports, and was thought for a very long time to be too strenuous for 'the weaker sex'. It was not until 1964 that the first female eventer competed at the Olympics. At that time Anne was fourteen and already mad about horses. It may have been this pioneering achievement that inspired Princess Anne to concentrate

'The horse is just about the only one who doesn't know I'm Royal'

Princess Anne

91

seriously on the most difficult discipline in equestrian sport. Eventing may also have been her choice because courage and vigour were her strong points. She enjoyed the danger and daring of riding cross-country. The patience of dressage just wasn't Princess Anne.

Her career began to blossom when she rode Doublet. In the summer of 1969, they won their very first novice hunter trial. The princess was still dividing her attention among three horses, but it was on Doublet, in 1971, that she qualified for the most prestigious British three-day event of the season, the Badminton horse trials.

That year the best of the British were there. So were the best of Europe. Princess Anne and Doublet finished a creditable fifth. Her prize was £150 and an invitation to compete at the European championships at Burghley.

But eight weeks before Burghley, she had to undergo what was then a difficult operation. She went into King Edward VII hospital to have an ovarian cyst removed. As for Burghley, everyone thought that was that. But Princess Anne was determined to ride in the championships. She went to a physiotherapist for exercises and walked miles in the Scottish hills near Balmoral to regain her fitness. Meanwhile, Alison Oliver put Doublet through his paces. Two weeks before Burghley, Princess Anne steeled herself to ride in the preliminary event.

Then came the championships. Princess Anne and Doublet, fresh from Oliver's pointers, were near-perfect in dressage; they won the day. But many doubted that so soon after an operation she could ride the gruelling cross-country phase. Rather than daunting Princess Anne, this speculation annoyed her. She wanted to show them. And she did. There was a hint of trouble at the Trout Hatchery, a water jump, but she won this phase too. After that, the showjumping must have seemed a doddle. Finishing with a clear round, she became the 1971 European champion. The Queen presented the trophy. Princess Anne was voted BBC Sports Personality of the Year by the British television audience.

But Doublet developed leg trouble.

Goodwill was to be her next horse. He was seven years old when Princess Anne got him, and had already been the champion working hunter at the Horse of the Year Show. He had been showjumped by a top rider. Nonetheless, there were problems: 'On occasion, I despaired of ever getting him to do anything in the dressage arena and his show-jumping proved fairly sketchy and erratic. But his cross-country was never any trouble,'[2] says Princess Anne.

At first, though, it was worrying because his centre of gravity was too far forward. 'It was very curious, my only problem was that he was so much on his forehand. I used to get very tired.' A rider's job is to get the horse to the fence in the right position; then it is up to the horse. By using a special bit, 'eventually Goodwill's centre of gravity was moved back a little.' This 'altered his whole way of crossing the country'. He moved with more economy, and his gallop was better.

At Badminton in 1973, Princess Anne and Goodwill finished fifth. Defending her title as an individual at the 1973 European championships in Kiev, she was again mounted on Goodwill. Early in the day, there were many falls at fence two, a wide spread over a deep ditch. 'I was told that the bank on the take-off side had given way a bit, that it was now slightly dangerous and that this had made the spread much bigger.' It was suggested that she jump the fence in a different way than she had walked it. She agreed to change her plan and 'quite simply got it wrong'.

On landing Goodwill tipped to one side, seemed about to regain his balance, but caught his hoof on the back pole of the fence and pitched forward on his nose. 'I decided that as Goodwill had hit the ground very hard, and I couldn't stand on one leg because it had gone numb and disappeared from my hip to my knee, that I certainly wasn't going to achieve anything by carrying on as I was not a member of the team. It was not a sensible policy to continue.'

The press, not knowing or not wanting to know the difference between team and individual riders, criticized her as a quitter. This further soured her already difficult relationship with reporters and photographers. But it did not sour her relationship with Goodwill.

The following year they finished fourth at Badminton and twelfth in the world championships at Burghley. Then they went as part of an all-woman British team to the 1975 European championships in Germany. These *Britischen Amazonen* were of course competing against men as well as other women. They took the team silver medal. The course was twisty, but Goodwill went well, and despite a horrid cold, Princess Anne won the individual silver medal. Another member of the team, Lucinda Prior-Palmer (now Lucinda Green), who was three years younger than the Princess, won the gold medal, mounted on a horse called Be Fair. Not surprisingly, both riders and their horses were chosen for the British team for the 1976 Olympics.

Charlemagne's six daughters, wearing divided skirts, rode with him. Throughout history women of noble birth have ridden horseback. Medieval tapestries show women out hunting with men. But it was not until 1952 that they were reluctantly allowed to compete with men in equestrian sport at the Olympics. That year four women took part in the dressage competition. One of them, Lis Hartel, a Dane who had had to relearn to ride after she was stricken with polio, won the silver medal; four years later she won it again.

But it was not until 1964 that Helena Dupont, an American, became the first woman to compete in an Olympic three-day event. At the next Games, in 1968, Jane Bullen, riding for Great Britain's winning team, became the first woman to share the team eventing gold medal. Women had won eventing medals at the world and European championships, they had been winning at Badminton and Burghley for some years, but no woman had yet won an individual Olympic three-day-event medal. Indeed, when Princess Anne and Lucinda Prior-Palmer arrived in Bromont, Canada, for the equestrian phase of the 1976 Montreal Olympics, there was still doubt in some people's minds about the suitability of three-day eventing for women. The cross-country phase, particularly, was dangerous.

Bromont was in ski country. It was fifty-three miles east of Montreal, and hilly. All of the equestrian athletes at the Games — the three-day eventers, the dressage teams and the showjumpers — were housed together in a mini Olympic Village. There were four hundred flats, or apartments, in the building, not really quite enough for the teams and their back-up, but they were all packed in. After the Games, the mini Olympic Village was to become low-cost housing. For their duration, seven hundred policemen and women, many with carbines, guarded the complex, and it was surrounded by a high fence. Not all of the security was for the Princess. At the previous Games, in Munich in 1972, Israeli athletes had been murdered by Palestinians. The Canadians were taking no chances.

Security was tight at the stable area too, which was more lavish than the premises for people. In fact, with one exception the stables were perfection. There was everything possible for the horses, and for the trainers there were such niceties as refrigerators filled with soft drinks. There was an abundance of practice areas and practice fences. The one flaw? The turf surrounding the stables had been sprayed to make it grow faster with a chemical that was poisonous to horses.[3]

The three-day event began, as usual, with the dressage. The crowd, the flags, that very special Olympic tension were unsettling to the horses. And to some of the riders. Many of the riders warmed up in the practice arena behind the collecting ring, hoping to get their horses used to the crowd, which was large because this was the Olympics and because there was a princess to see. When Princess Anne and Goodwill were performing their dressage test, the crowd watched in silence but intently, though not as intently as the cameras. Goodwill, brimming with energy, broke from the trot to a canter twice, and they ended halfway down the list with a penalty score of 91.25. When Princess Anne rode stiffly out of the arena, half the crowd left too.

Lucinda Prior-Palmer had a better dressage test; at the end of that part of the three-day event she was in fifth place. Dressage had never been Princess's Anne's forte. She and Goodwill had made the Olympic team because of their ability riding cross-country.

The very twisty course, with its ground changes, its bumps, sharp corners and hills looked easy to many. But the oldest hands were wary. After walking the course, General Prior-Palmer, an experienced horseman, shook his head at the thought of 'that hill at the beginning,' concluding, 'It's a very tough course.' Nor was he the only one who thought and said so.

The course had been designed by the foremost course builder in Canada, Barbara Kemp. She had been one of the first Canadians to be smitten by the sport. It happened to her in 1951 at Badminton. The following year and every year thereafter, she had designed a course in Canada. By trade, Kemp was an administration officer at Montreal General Hospital. Expert course building was an avocation.

To get the best sense of Bromont's natural slope Barbara Kemp skied it during the winter. For the summer, she added some strange gradients and some ingenious 'fences'. There were always alternative ways of taking a fence; the shortest, quickest route was always the hardest one. 'I tried to build the course so that a bad horse could jump a safer way round for more time faults,' Barbara Kemp said. 'However, I had no guarantee that the rider of a less-good horse would have the sense to take the safest route.'[4]

Kemp had kept two factors particularly in mind in deciding where to site the fences. 'The first consideration has got to be the horse. The second consideration must be the public, because if you have no spectacle, you have no sport,' she said. Therefore there

'The main thing is the horse must have confidence in you'

Eventer Rachel Hunt, 1987

were groups of fences. They 'help viewers,' she said, 'and also give a horse a chance to catch its breath, a change of pace to get its second wind.'

Unseasonable rain three weeks before the Games softened the ground, making the tricky Olympic course harder to ride safely. More rain might cause nasty complications. The night before the cross-country phase was to begin the storm swept down from the hills.

At 8 am, when the first horse and rider set off, there were clouds lurking over the Canadian hilltops, but it was hardly raining at all. Rider after rider set off, aware that another storm was gathering force.

The clouds burst as Princess Anne's turn came. She mounted and set off cross-country in blinding rain.

At fence two, where horse and rider came upon a rail fence at the very bottom of a steep bank, a crowd had gathered expecting spills. Princess Anne and Goodwill jumped it.

Course designer Barbara Kemp

At fence eight, on the logging trail, the obstacle loomed suddenly and unexpectedly on an uphill turn. Eight horses refused. Princess Anne and Goodwill jumped, and galloped on. But clearly this was not at all Goodwill's sort of course. He performed best on big, open courses. But despite the intricate terrain – and the weather – they were going quickly and surprisingly well.

At fence ten, called the Slalom, Princess Anne and Goodwill faced a twisting three-jump course that sloped downhill at unlikely angles. That fence, which has been called 'a brute of ingenuity', was the site of most of the day's upsets. Princess Anne pulled Goodwill back to a hand canter, and they jumped and were over safely.

But at fence nineteen, a zigzag over a ditch, Goodwill stumbled in the takeoff ground, which had become boggy. Momentarily, his hooves stuck in the mud, causing him to mis-step. 'It wasn't that hideous a fence; you could kick on,' says Princess Anne. 'The last thing I remember was seeing my stride and that it was wrong. So he was then left with one and a half strides instead of two and was going too fast to be able to do anything about it. After the inevitable sinking feeling I have no further recollection of what happened. I knew it would be disaster.'[5]

Horse and rider fell on the landing side of the fence. Goodwill had managed to jump the fence, and Princess Anne to hang on, but then the horse lost his footing entirely, and fell heavily. Princess Anne's head struck the ground. The horse pulled himself upright. He had

lost a shoe. Some witnesses say that the rider was knocked out, and lay on the ground unconscious for nearly five minutes. All agreed she was concussed. When she could stand up, she felt bruised, dizzy and dazed. With effort, Princess Anne remounted. If the British team was to stay in contention, she had to finish the course.

It would not be easy. There were seventeen fences remaining, none of them doddles. Eight riders were eliminated in the water (fences 22–24), where horse and rider so often part the ways. Princess Anne and Goodwill took the jumps in stride, then heaved themselves onto the bank and kept going.

On the last fence, three foot two inches high and four feet wide, the Canadian Cathy Wedge mounted on City Fella, who had been clear till then, tripped. Princess Anne rode to the finish. At the finish she was found to be medically concussed. Her first memory is

Princess Anne galloping, just after her fall, Bromont, Canada, 1976

of having her boots pulled off in the stables about fifteen minutes after passing the finishing post. She had shown great courage.

And Lucinda Prior-Palmer had had a clear cross-country round. The British looked set to go into the last event, the showjumping, in second place. But it was not to be.

If the day had been disastrous for Princess Anne, it was to be tragic for Lucinda Prior-Palmer and Be Fair. During the cross-country, Be Fair had slipped a tendon on his hock, and was declared unsound. Not only was he out of the Olympics, but his days in top competition were over. Four years later that weak tendon snapped and the horse, which had spent its last years hunting, was in pain and had to be shot.

A second British horse had also been found to be unsound after the cross-country, and the British team was eliminated. Princess Anne's courageous ride had been in vain.

The last day of competition was showjumping. She put in a clear round, finishing the Games in twenty-fourth place.

They always hit a woman when she is down. Now it was said she had made the team only because she was the Queen's daughter. That must have hurt, but it was not true. The Princess had been European champion and European silver medallist. Who else to name to the Olympic team? Her twenty-fourth place at the Olympics had been a painful result. Would she take comfort eight years later when the record showed that the American rider Karen Stives, who came to the fore at the 1984 Los Angeles Olympics, had been twenty-fifth at the equally important world championships?

'Hamish and I have been given a tiny flat by Mummy next to the stables'

Virginia Holgate of her wedding plans

California, 1984. It was hot. You could see the cool mountains in the distance, as you stood in the lovely natural amphitheatre of the Santa Anita racecourse, which was the focal point for equestrian events at the Olympics. The grooms were sweltering in the heat; the horses too. Most of the electric fans were put into service to cool the horses. Although the racecourse was apparently a heat trap, the British rider Virginia Holgate (later Leng) was impressed with its conditions for the horses: 'There was every facility we could possibly require – for schooling, jumping, galloping or for a relaxed hack around the outside of the racecourse.'[6]

Conditions were favourable to riders too: 'By the time the horses had been returned to their stables after their early morning exercise, we were more than ready to do justice to the incredible breakfast which the organizers had prepared for us.' Namely, 'fresh melons, strawberries, a selection of cereals, Danish pastries, scrambled egg, potato cakes, bacon, sausages, tomatoes, toast and croissants . . .'

Except for the heat and some awkwardness during the first acclimatization week because owners were barred from the stables, it looked set to be a good Olympics. After considerable negotiation, the Olympic authorities relented, and owners were admitted.

The dressage and showjumping phases of the three-day event were to take place at Santa Anita. But the cross-country course had been built one hundred miles south, at Fairbanks Ranch near San Diego, where the climate was supposed to be cooler. It was hot.

In the eight years since the Canada Olympics, the eventing scene had changed thoroughly. Princess Anne had honourably retired an ageing Goodwill in 1979; he was fourteen. She did not, unfortunately, have another top-flight eventing horse, and she was often busy with royal duties. (What no one suspected was that in 1986 and 1987 she would make another small dent in riding history, though not at the Olympics, as a jockey.)

Lucinda Prior-Palmer was now Lucinda Green. She was acknowledged as the finest woman rider in the world, and had she been a man, she would have been regarded as the finest rider in the world. At the 1982 world championships, the last before these Olympics, Green had ridden Regal Realm, and won the individual and team gold medal. She won the Badminton International six times, each time on a different horse, and she took the European championship twice.

But her success had never been reflected at the Olympics. In 1976, in Canada, she had had to withdraw when Be Fair injured his tendon. In 1980, at the alternate Olympics, in France, she finished seventh on Village Gossip. In 1984, mounted on Regal Realm, she hoped at last to win a medal at the Olympics.

There was now another notable British rider, Virginia Holgate, who was twenty-nine, two years younger than Lucinda Green. She had shared in the team gold medals at the 1981 European championships and at the 1982 world championship.

Holgate had fallen in 1976, breaking her left arm in twenty-three places. There had been talk of amputation; then two four-hour operations. The nerves of her arm were damaged, and thought irreparable. The arm was horribly bent, crooked at right angles to her body, utterly useless. One day, a veterinarian who had come to examine the horses had a look at the X-rays of her arm, and then suddenly grabbed hold of it and pulled it nearly straight. The

moment had been painful, but it had resurrected her riding career. Now most of the feeling had returned to her arm; she was riding well; she had had plenty of years to get over the scare of the accident.

Not so the American rider Karen Stives, who was obviously talented, but who had had a bad fall only two years earlier, in 1982. Born in Wellesley, Massachusetts, Stives had been riding since the age of seven. Her favourite aspect of three-day eventing was cross-country. In her view, 'It's a real high.' But just two years before the Olympics, Stives had had a terrible accident at the Kentucky Three-Day Event, when her horse Silent Partner fell on her.

It was thought she might have to give up competing entirely, but only three months later she rode The Saint at the 1982 world championships. It was then that she had finished twenty-fifth. Stives had indeed lost, but she was not defeated. She immediately bought another horse, Ben Arthur. He had been ridden by another rider at those same championships and finished an ignominious thirty-ninth.

The following June, Stives and Ben Arthur were third at the prestigious Kentucky meeting. And now they were at the Olympics.

Women had been barred from Olympic three-day eventing for as long as possible. In 1984, only twenty years since the first lone woman had barged in, fully eighteen of the forty-eight riders in the three-day event were female.

On the night before the cross-country, more than one rider sat down with the map of the course and a tape recorder in front of her, recording absolutely everything she could remember about each fence – the slope of the terrain, the number of trees, where best to turn.

Virginia Holgate was to be the first British rider over the course. That was the worst spot. It meant she had to take the fences without any information from her teammates; but she would be a useful voice of experience for them. The Fairbanks Ranch where the alarming cross-country course had been built had once belonged to the Hollywood movie idol Douglas Fairbanks. There was plenty of acting going on too on the morning of the cross-country. It was the only way to hide nervousness, which might be catching, from your teammates and from the horses.

The day was very hot. It was like riding through a sauna. The dry grass was surprisingly slick on the turns. Virginia Holgate was pleased when she finished the course with only a 0.4 penalty.

Virginia Holgate Leng, bronze medallist in three-day eventing at the 1984 Olympics

101

Lucinda Green had a fast, clear round. Indeed, she was one of only three riders who had neither jumping nor time penalties, but because she had been harshly marked in the dressage test, she was definitely out of the medals.

At the end of the cross-country, the American team was poised for the team gold, and in the individual competition, to her own surprise, Karen Stives on Ben Arthur was the rider in gold medal position. To win, they would have to have a clear round on the final day of competition, in the showjumping. New Zealander Mark Todd was lying a close second on Charisma, and Virginia Holgate was third on Priceless. No woman had ever won any individual medal at the Olympic three-day event. Now two, Stives and Holgate, were in contention.

The showjumping takes place in reverse order of standing. Green went clear on Regal Realm; her final Olympic placing was sixth. When Holgate's turn came; she too went clear. She knew she had a medal. Next came Mark Todd. He went clear. If Karen Stives finished in either first or second position, and barring disaster she would, Holgate's medal would be bronze.

Because she was the points leader so far, Karen Stives was the last rider. Ever since the cross-country had finished, Stives had been the one under the pressure. If she hit just one fence, she would lose the gold medal. Ben Arthur was not a terribly reliable showjumper. She did not expect to win.

The tension was palpable as Stives and Ben Arthur began the showjumping round. What an upset it would be if she were to win. To avoid becoming a nervous wreck, Stives pretended to herself that this was a very ordinary occasion, in which she was jumping at home.

They had gone into the arena to get it over with. But Stives was controlling Ben Arthur's approach to each fence perfectly, and he was jumping with care and courage. It looked as though she was going to get that gold medal.

But suddenly, a fence was down. There were oohs from the sympathetic crowd. And then cheers: she had won an Olympic silver medal. Holgate had her bronze. Like nearly every other winner before her, Karen Stives said, 'He's the best horse I've ever ridden.'

Karen Stives on Ben Arthur riding the cross-country course at the 1984 Olympics

'History is being made. The world champion is a woman'

Television commentator, when Gail Greenough won the 1986 world showjumping championship

CHAPTER 8

SOAR LIKE AN EAGLE, SOAR, SOAR

*T*he sun of Jamaica. The peanut farms. Bare feet. Mango trees. Her friends. Her Gran who has raised her. Everything will have to be left behind when nine-year-old Tessa Sanderson boards the plane to join her parents in England.[1] She hides in the Jamaica hills to avoid leaving. But is found, taken to Montego Bay airport, and put firmly on the plane. Fourteen hours later, young Tessa arrives in England, in dark, icy, morning sleet.

Nothing in her life would ever compare with that very reluctant departure, that wrench of circumstance, in the early spring of 1965. Not even the reality of prejudice: 'Within days of starting my new school one white boy, and I can still remember his name, called me all sorts of names and spat on my brand new uniform.' It got worse. A girl, refusing to return a pair of training shoes, jeered, 'You black wog.'[2]

Life in the Midlands of industrial England was all that Tessa Sanderson had feared. But she was gifted at sport; she had the encouragement of hard-working parents; she was lucky in her coach. She persevered in her chosen sport, the javelin, and began to win – gold in 1978 at the Commonwealth Games, followed by silver at the European championships. That raised everyone's expectations, including her own. But in Moscow at the 1980 Olympics, which should have been the summit of her career, Tessa Sanderson froze and failed even to qualify for the Olympic final.

By the winter of 1982, she had regained her confidence. Then came a terrible injury. She tore her Achilles tendon during a club race, and when she fell, landed on the elbow of her throwing arm, which cracked. That kept her out of the European championships and the next Commonwealth Games. She was supposed to be as good as new at the 1983 world championships, but finished only fourth – out of the medals. 'Being second', the saying goes, 'ain't no good at all.'

Being fourth was worse. You couldn't live on it, and you certainly couldn't get a job on it – at Sanderson's age, twenty-eight in the Olympic year of 1984, her post-javelin career was of concern, particularly as her Olympic prospects were considered nil or poor. The press, who had watched her closely, now had their eye on the other British Javelin thrower, Fatima Whitbread, who was five years younger than Sanderson, and getting better with every throw. Whitbread had thrown well enough at the European championships to displace Sanderson from the top of the United Kingdom rankings for the first time in a decade. Then she had won silver at the world championships. She was the up-and-comer. Sanderson, any sports writer would tell you, was past it, a has-been. They had even, in so many words, told Sanderson.

Tessa Sanderson's coach Wilf Paish, a dapper little man with a moustache, still believed in her. She tried to believe in herself. When 'you overcome your problems', Sanderson told herself, you get 'a layer of strength within you that, as Boy Scouts say, will help you overcome all difficulties'. Only Los Angeles would tell.

Would she even qualify for the 1984 Olympic final? Or would there be a repeat of Moscow, stage fright, a 'rubbishy' throw? To the surprise of many, she did throw well enough to qualify for the Olympic final. But few believed she could win an Olympic medal.

The weather on the day of the final was almost Jamaican. It was hot. But it was choking, smoggy, Los Angeles hot. Her coach Wilf Paish was there to prime her for the final. He shook her hand to make it loose, and gave her the usual pre-competition kiss on the cheek. Now she was on her own.

The stifling day began to turn to a blue, more breathable evening. There was only a faint breeze. Tessa Sanderson knew she would have to throw high and dead centre to float the javelin on so gentle a current of air. She stripped off her warmups, stretched, picked up the javelin, and began to run. 'My last thought before the run-up was "please God, make it right."' Then she said silently, 'Come on, Tessa, get it right now, just hit hard.' She was running fast, holding the javelin high, her body square, and then, she hurled the javelin. She knew instantly that it was a long throw. But she had let it go a metre before the disqualification line. Would the throw be long enough? As though wishing would make it so, she said, over and over and over, 'Make it near 70 and everyone will have to fight.'

The javelin bounced to the ground just short of 70 metres, at the 69.56 metre mark. That was a metre further than Wilf Paish had estimated would be necessary for victory in that still air. She felt elation. Then she reminded herself that there were six rounds of throws; and everyone had hopes. 'Stay cool,' she told herself.

By the end of that first round, Sanderson was still leading. In the second round, though, Fatima Whitbread crept close with 65.42 metres. Then the tall, lean world champion, Tiina Lillak, a Finn, let go a knock-out throw. Only the year before, in 1983, Lillak had shattered the world record with a throw that verged on 75 metres. Could she do it today? Had she just done it?

Fatima Whitbread, 1984 bronze medallist, congratulating Tessa Sanderson on her Olympic victory

Tessa Sanderson was a thousand jangling nerve endings as she waited for the electronic scoreboard to record the distance. It was a good throw, far, 69.00, but not far enough. Lillak had injured her ankle, and took no more throws. Fatima Whitbread kept trying, and on her fifth throw of the competition, moved into bronze medal position with 67.14. She was getting a second wind. Would she, Tessa Sanderson wondered, put it all together on her last throw of the competition? Or would Sanderson herself prevail?

Throughout the competition Tessa Sanderson had used concentration techniques to focus her attention; these mind games were and are the rage. Before each throw, before the 'please Gods' entered her head, she had been taught to say to herself: 'You are the best in the world. You are the best technically . . . Soar like an eagle, soar, soar.'

She had soared. Would Fatima Whitbread soar higher? Sanderson felt her body going cold as she waited for the sixth and last throw. The stadium was now floodlit. The crowd was as tense as she was. Fatima Whitbread threw. But she couldn't better her javelin mark, she had bronze. Tiina Lillak had won silver.

Tessa Sanderson fell to her knees and made a two-armed gesture of triumph. 'Me! Olympic champion, Olympic record-breaker, first British girl to win a throwing event, fourth since the war to win an athletics gold, first black girl to win a throwing gold. And I was in heaven.' A British fan leaped over the fence, kissed her, and said, 'Tessa, you're a darling.'

Fatima Whitbread could not help herself. She wept. And then she congratulated Tessa Sanderson. The 1988 Seoul Olympics, Fatima Whitbread had to hope, would belong to her. She has come a long way since Los Angeles.

In the summer of 1986, in a nearly empty stadium in West Germany, she hurled her javelin into the history books, becoming the first woman to throw a javelin over 250 feet. Her throw was 77.44 metres (254 feet). No one had thought a woman would ever throw so far. That triumph ended in the best possible manner a year of disappointment and heartache on and off the competition field.

Nearly the only people in the stadium the day Whitbread set that new world record in a qualifying round for the European championships were other javelin throwers. The greatest thrower of the previous generation, the East German Ruth Fuchs was there with her protégée Petra Felke. It was Felke's world record that Whitbread

'These fireworks, Tessa, they're all for you'

Edwin Moses at post-Olympic celebration

107

shattered. Felke said she was less surprised than Fatima Whitbread at the gargantuan throw. 'I always thought that Fatima had got one or two really big throws in her. But I still think I can win the European championship.' In fact, Whitbread won it the next day.

'People think of me as the incredible hulk'

Fatima Whitbread

The irony was that if she had been born in East Germany instead of in England, Fatima Whitbread would not have become the European and a year later the world javelin champion. Sports scientists would have channelled her into another, more suitable sport because theoretically she just wasn't big enough for the javelin.

The cameras lie. 'People think of me as the incredible hulk,' Fatima Whitbread says, flashing the broad grin that is not yet as famous as her tears. 'When people see me in the flesh they are surprised at how small I am.' A few inches taller, the pundits used to groan, and she would be unbeatable. Hers is a case – increasingly rare in sport – of will overcoming anatomy.

Those muscles are there all right, but they hang on a mere five-foot four-inch frame. This makes them look even bigger than they are. It also makes them crucial. Whitbread's strongest rival, still the long-limbed East German Petra Felke, is five foot eight. Even that other British shorty Tessa Sanderson, the 1984 Olympic champion, stands more than five foot six. And the lanky ex-world champion, Tiina Lillak, the Finn whose title Fatima Whitbread took in the Coliseum at Rome, is a powerful five foot eleven.

In Los Angeles in 1984, Whitbread, having just recovered from a fibroid operation, won a disappointing bronze medal. At last, in the September sun of Rome, at the 1987 world championships, Fatima Whitbread triumphed. Even though she had less time than her opponents to acclimatize to the humidity and heat; even though she was nursing a painful, temporarily gimpy arm and shoulder with cortisone injections. Small wonder that 'It felt like pulling tusks from an elephant'.

Great wonder, she won. 'I stood on the victory platform and listened while they played the national anthem. I was tired and my arm ached but I had never felt better in my life.'

The habit of surmounting adversity goes back to her less than lovely childhood. Abandoned as a baby in Hackney, she grew up in children's homes, with no mainstay, no direction, no prospects. Not surprisingly, twelve-year-old Fatima was so disruptive, so difficult, that PE teacher Margaret Whitbread, a former British

World champion: Fatima Whitbread elated, Rome, 1987

javelin international, was far from delighted when Fatima first turned up at javelin practice.

But the javelin is the stuff of classical mythology, a magical implement. If television used its nous and spliced the javelin competition together, showing it as a whole instead of in disjointed bits and pieces, it would make transfixing viewing. You would feel the tension building. The javelin captured young Fatima's imagination, and that changed her life.

Never had Margaret Whitbread had so dedicated a young athlete to coach. Never had Fatima had such intense attention. One of Mrs Whitbread's sons suggested his parents adopt Fatima. Fatima had had to wait nearly fourteen years to get what most children have from the start, a family.

Now, with her mother-coach behind her, Fatima Whitbread began the journey to the top of the javelin world. 'Early on,' Margaret Whitbread says, 'at competitions, we used to watch stealthily when the East Germans were training, in order to pick up a few tips they didn't want to give us. Now we know better what we are doing.'

'I don't dislike my muscles. I enjoy feeling healthy, looking good'

Fatima Whitbread

With Fatima Whitbread's beginning in life, it was no big deal for her at the age of twenty-six to defy fate on a small matter like the world championships. Her victory against the odds made Whitbread the most talked about woman in Britain. Whitbread was invited to 10 Downing Street. She was voted by the public BBC Sports Personality of the Year.

It was a joyous moment. But as Fatima Whitbread, with her polka-dot dress slit to the thigh, walked up to collect the Sports Personality of the Year award, and the commentator spoke of 'the year of the wiggle', the moment was dismaying too. It had been the year of the win, not the wiggle. The woman was a champion, not a vamp.

Why should it be necessary (and it had been necessary) for her to invent a victory wiggle, or to pose for glamorized fashion photographs in the tabloid of tabloids, the *Sun*? Why is it enough for champions like Steve Cram merely to win? If, like Sebastian Coe, they do appear in clothing ads, it is not to sell themselves but to sell the clothes.

Fatima Whitbread and many other women feel it necessary to show off their so-called sex appeal, feminize their image, because we don't like muscles on our women. Sponsors prefer bustlines to biceps. But, Catch 22, to hurl the javelin across world record shattering distances, you need muscles that show.

Whitbread trains relentlessly – seven days a week, three, four times a day to build those muscles. She is at ease with them. But we are not. Fatima Whitbread, wanting only to be on the front line of her sport, to win, finds herself also on the frontier of conventional notions about femininity. It is dangerous territory, full of snipers. The pentathlete Mary Peters has been there. So has the equestrian Princess Anne. It is a great unfairness that women champions not only have to overcome the pressures of top-level sport, but also the pressures of prejudice – and innuendo about drug abuse.

'The first thing I heard when I came home from Rome was a reporter saying, Do you take drugs? I've been tested five times this year, winter as well as summer. I even put myself in for a test at a meeting where I wasn't competing to set an example.'

Fatima Whitbread, 1984 Olympic bronze medalist, is on the eve of the 1988 Olympics Britain's best-known sportswoman and probably the finest javelin thrower in the world. The one other woman thought capable of winning the javelin championship is the tall East German Petra Felke. Felke regained the world record in the summer of 1987, but that autumn Whitbread beat Felke in Rome at the world championships.

There is friendship between rivals in their case. To the big athletics gala in Monte Carlo which followed the world championships, Whitbread brought some chic Western clothes, includ-

Petra Felke

'I knew Fatima could do it'

Petra Felke

ing a leather jacket, to give as a gift to Felke. 'They can't get everything they like in East Germany,' Whitbread said. 'I had promised Petra I would find some things for her.' A delighted Felke gave her a traditional German wooden doll. But their sports rivalry continued unabated.

With her 77.44-metre throw in 1986, Whitbread broke a psychological barrier in her sport (throwing over 250 feet). Now, like Petra Felke, she wants to be the first to throw over 80 metres – perhaps at the 1988 Seoul Olympics.

A gold medal there would make Fatima Whitbread the first woman ever to achieve the triple – the European, world, and Olympic titles – sometimes called the javelin grand slam. Because Whitbread is Whitbread, the odds are on her side.

Fatima Whitbread wanted to be the best in the world, to win an Olympic medal, to set a world record, to be world champion. She has attained all that, and is striving for more in her sport.

Whitbread grew up with the knowledge she would have to be tough, have to go for it herself, if anything was to become of her. It is the lesson that boys get, not the more usual one for girls: be independent but not too independent. Then, when she was at last tucked into the bosom of the Whitbread family, Fatima Whitbread received that nurturance that men so often get from mothers and girlfriends and wives. Margaret Whitbread perhaps felt freer to mother Fatima differently because she was also occupying another traditional nurturing role, that of coach. Wilf Paish occupied that role for Tessa Sanderson.

As psychologists have come to understand over the last few years, it is rare that mothers feel free to give that unbridling, unhindering nurturance to daughters. There is often the subtext to the lesson, the message, be a little careful, a little subservient, a little girl.

What women want and need is nurturance and encouragement toward autonomy, toward being independent. What we need, all of us, is a coach. It is not surprising that so many female athletes wind up marrying their coach.

The coach's role is intimate and loving. She or he gives instruction and teaches self-reliance. And because winning in sport requires the same skills, the same self-mastery and confidence of both sexes, no competent coach would under-cut the message with the self-defeating subtext of antiquated femininity. The coach is the quintessential Good Mother, whose role is to help athletes soar.

CHAPTER 9

COLLISION COURSE

As the barefoot runner who led the race ran the last lap, the excited crowd in Stellenbosch stadium began to chant, 'Zo-La, Zo-La, Zo-La, Zo-la.' As she crossed the finish line, shattering the world 5,000 metres record by an astonishing six seconds, the rhythmic chant became a loud, exuberant cheer. On that South African summer's day in January 1984, small, slight Zola Budd, who was seventeen but who looked younger, was anointed an Afrikaner heroine.

But Mary Decker had nothing to worry about yet, even though it was her 15-minute, 8.26-second record which Budd had broken. Decker was the pre-eminent middle-distance runner in the world. Pop-star thin, with a history of defeating the Russians, she was America's favourite runner, and she was just twenty-five, in her athletic prime. She had other records chalked up. And because of the boycott of South African sport, the new 15-minute, 1.83-second world 5,000-metre mark would never be entered in the record books. Records set in South Africa could not be ratified. South African teams and athletes were barred from major sporting events, including the Olympics.

Zola Budd, who hailed from Bloemfontein in the heart of Afrikanerdom, was happy in *Suid Afrika*. She did not despise apartheid. But so long as she held a South African passport, she could never be world or European or Olympic champion. Just three months after Stellenbosch, she left for London. Two weeks later she was a British citizen.

It did not go unnoticed that in the United Kingdom, where immigration officials appear to make a great effort to stay years behind on paperwork, the application of this white South African,

'Zola looks like a twelve year old, runs like a twenty-five year old, and is only seventeen. She's unbelievable'

Ingrid Kristiansen

who saw no reason to speak out against apartheid, had been pushed to the top. Four days after arriving in London, Laatlammetjie, as Zola Budd was called by her parents – in Afrikaans it means late lamb – had applied for citizenship. Ten days later, on 6 April, after the intervention of the Home Secretary, she learned that her application had been approved.

The House of Commons was told that 'failure to give her priority would have been unreasonable'. Why? Because the 1984 Olympics were looming. A young athlete's potential ought not to be blighted, the argument went, and she would run in British colours – a 'British' chance of gold ought not to be lost. Until her eighteenth birthday on 26 May, Budd could be granted citizenship as a dependent child. Her maternal forebears were Afrikaner *Voortrek-kers*, but Zola Budd's father's father had been born in London. Because her parents were putting on the charade of settling in England before her birthday, Zola Budd could qualify as a dependent child. Later, it would take years longer. The 1988 Los Angeles Olympics would have come and gone. A talented runner would have been denied an opportunity to run. The 'British' opportunity for victory would have been lost.

The world's quarrel, it was argued, was with the South African government, not with individual sportswomen and sportsmen. A number of sports figures had emigrated to be eligible for international competition. The black South African Sidney Maree had become an American citizen; his naturalization had taken the statutory four years, but in the meantime he had been able to compete.

The case was even made that Budd's defection would further undermine South African sport. This was a cynical lie. Her victory could benefit only South Africa and the circulation of the London tabloid, the *Daily Mail*, which offered exclusive inside information on her whereabouts, her training programme, her loyalties: 'Zola Budd will become a great British athlete . . . her heart lies here.'

Surely few people in power were taken in by this propaganda: the then British Minister for Sport, Neil Macfarlane, later admitted: 'I had no doubts that if she were to run for Britain in Los Angeles and if she were to win a gold medal, when she stood on the rostrum, with the national anthem echoing round the stadium, people would identify her as a South African running for this country.'[1] The Olympics have always been viewed as a showcase for national aspiration. There is no separating sport from politics, most particularly not in the case of Zola Budd.

Zola Budd makes the headlines

Denying her application would have been politically responsible. Perhaps it would have been sad for Budd herself. Perhaps not – a gargantuan Olympic fiasco was looming. What is certain is that politics had made Zola Budd a special case and would continue to do so. She could never be just a runner with potential who wanted to compete against the best. She was a symbol of racism. And throughout the years that followed she ignored every opportunity – and there were many – to distance herself from apartheid.

And yet it was hard to equate her with evil. That delicate bone structure made her appear even smaller than she was. Publicly, she was shy, self-effacing; she seemed to be so young, so innocent. She was stereotypically feminine in demeanour, and in her sport, she was sweetly brave: a front runner, who could run serenely but very fast, seemingly unaware of the frantic pack of runners at her heel. Zola Budd's hair was more brown in colour than blonde. Nonetheless she was a Golden Girl.

And they are few and far between. She so perfectly fitted a cultural stereotype, she was – except for that inopportune link with South Africa – an ideal type. Tradition's favourite. An old-fashioned girl. Yet she could run – and there was money in that, and national prestige. The *Mail* and the government sensed they were on to a winner, whether she actually won at the Olympics or not. Thus, the government decided to turn a blind eye to her little foible, racism.

The lobbying of powerful interests, greed for Olympic gold, and the endearing fact that she was in most respects a Golden Girl, convinced a Conservative government – which allegedly embraced the traditional values of *Kinder*, *Kirche*, *Küche* (children, church, kitchen) – to move offical mountains for a sports*woman*.

Was it progress? Whatever it was, Mary Decker now had a personal interest in Zola Budd's career. Budd would be there at the Olympics. The political decision to rush through her British citizenship had set Zola Budd and Mary Decker on a collision course.

Mary Decker was not unduly frightened of up-and-coming, seventeen-year-old Budd. Decker herself had been a running prodigy, a younger prodigy, nationally famous at fourteen. Now she was the most famous woman runner in the United States. Even intellectuals knew her name. Even traditionalists (read male chauvinist pigs) approved of her: she ran in earrings and a necklace and what looked like mascara. She was as fine-boned as Zola Budd and leggier, and she was the world champion at 1,500 and 3,000 metres.

Decker would celebrate her twenty-sixth birthday one week before the 1984 Olympics. She planned to give herself a late present, the first ever 3,000-metres Olympic title. She had set world records at 5,000 and 10,000 metres, but 3,000 metres was the longest distance women could then run at the Olympics, except for the 26-mile 385-yard marathon, which was also making its debut for women at Los Angeles. Because there were so few distances for women to choose from at the Olympics, it was likely that Zola Budd would be running in Mary Decker's race.

But so too would Maricica Puica of Romania and Wendy Sly of Britain, and there were other good contenders. Even so, Mary Decker, the fastest woman in the world in middle-distance running, fitter than ever and faster too, was odds-on favourite to win the Olympic championship.

Her feats on the track had been news since 1973 when, at the age of fourteen years 224 days, she became the youngest American ever to compete in an international track event. The sportswriters had liked her pigtails and called her 'Little Mary'. Before her fifteenth birthday, she outraced a Russian at 800 metres in the Soviet town of Minsk, and was applauded as an American heroine, a soldier on the sports front of the Cold War.

Decker's early history is the stuff of kiddie legend. She was eleven, so the story goes, living with her family in California, when she and a friend saw a leaflet advertising a cross-country race in the city park. Without knowing quite what cross-country was, they entered. Little Mary won.

In Long Beach, California, she became a running starlet, the way girls in Hollywood longed to become movie starlets.

For the Long Beach Comets, her running club, she raced hard — three or four times a weekend. During one wondrous and punishing week when she was just twelve, Decker ran a marathon and the 440, 880 and the mile, finishing with a two-mile race. The next day she had an appendectomy. 'No, I wasn't ever pushed,' she insists. 'I would train hard and race hard because that was me. It was something within myself.'

At about this time, she began to set records for her age group. But she didn't make it to the 1976 Olympics. Injury struck. 'By the time I was sixteen, I was a has-been,' Decker says. When she was

'The more I win, the more I want to win'

Mary Decker Slaney

seventeen – Zola Budd's age – she had to give up running completely. She could hardly walk. The pain in her calf muscles was agony.

'At sixteen I was already a has been'

Mary Decker Slaney

If she could not run, she could be around runners. Decker enrolled at the University of Colorado in Boulder. It was a runner's mecca. There she met Dick Quax, the 1976 Olympic 5,000-metre silver medallist from New Zealand. Quax had had similar problems with his legs, and had been cured by surgery. He had had the very operation that the first of the dozens of doctors Decker had been to see had recommended to her. Many New Zealand athletes, Quax said, had undergone the operation.

Mary Decker's problem was caused at least partly by training too much too soon. A runner's calf muscles grow big through training. This causes pain when the sheaths of tissue surrounding the muscles don't keep up – if they are too small they constrict the muscle. The answer is for the surgeon to slit the sheaths; the athlete exercises her calf; and scar tissue grows around the incisions making the sheaths large enough to hold the muscle without causing pain.

Decker had the operation on both of her legs in 1977. Two weeks later, she jogged half a mile. A year later, after four years off the track, she set a world indoor record for 1,000 yards. 'It was wonderful. I was so happy. That awful pain was gone.'

Unfortunately, the pain came back. A second operation on her left leg, in August of 1978, finally did the trick. And, uncharacteristically, she agreed to take things gently. She ran only thirteen miles a day, trained in the morning and late in the afternoon, and began to have many fewer injuries. She was asked to join Athletics West, the elite runners' 'club', which Nike, the sport shoe and clothing manufacturers, ran in that other American runner's town, Eugene, Oregon. She would go there to prepare for the 1980 Olympics.

There are pine trees in Eugene, and clean air. The climate is unlike South Africa and certainly unlike England. At Athletics West, a number of top athletes lived, trained, were massaged and monitored. In those days, runners were still supposed to be amateurs. 'Shamateurism' was in its heyday. Sport would soon go open, but because it hadn't yet, Nike employed Mary Decker as a 'saleswoman' and donated the services of a psychologist, a physiologist, the masseur who gave Athletics West club members hour-long massages twice a week, coaching as required, and shoes and sports clothing. The athletes lived together companionably, in groups of four or five, in large, rambling Oregon houses, where there was always plenty of muesli in the cupboard, and usually a row of muddy running shoes lined up near the door. At Decker's place, there was also carrot cake on the table – her own recipe. The athletes Decker shared the house with were all male. Of the twenty-nine Athletics West club members in 1980, when I went to Oregon to see her, Mary Decker was the only woman.

That didn't surprise or worry her. Prize money wasn't equal either. She had recently broken another world record and was paid, she told me – though absolutely not for publication then; it was still illegal – an under-the-table bonus of $3,000 (£2,000). The male star Henry Rono's fee for setting world records, Decker said, was $6,000. When payments to athletes became legal the $3,000 she spoke of would seem a pittance. Five years later, in tight-fisted London, she would receive $75,000 for running against Zola Budd in a race where there was no prospect of a world record.

In 1980, when the United States government decided to boycott the Moscow Olympics, Little Mary, who had become America's Sweetheart, became for many, Mary, Mary, Quite Contrary. All over the United States and in Britain and in the other nations that boycotted Moscow, athletes felt they had been betrayed. Their years of training had become a calculated cost of the Cold War. They felt rage. Decker voiced it. Her forthright and angry opposition to the American boycott of the Moscow Games was reported world-wide. But many people disapproved of her open anger. They thought this honest expression of views strident; unfeminine.

Unconsciously, Decker turned the anger in upon herself: she began to overtrain again, and although she knew how to keep it in good repair, she soon strained her Achilles tendon. Not only couldn't she run, she couldn't walk except with crutches.

But by 1982, she was off and running again, well enough to set world records that summer at 5,000 and 10,000 metres. In 1983, in Helsinki, at the first World Athletics Championships, fierce front running won her the 1,500 and the 3,000 metres titles. She was double world champion. The only thing that could top that was an Olympic gold medal.

The Olympic confrontation between Zola Budd and Mary Decker came, at last, on 10 August 1984 in the Los Angeles Coliseum, where they faced each other in the 3,000-metres final, seven and a

> **'What's the use of doing something if you don't try to be the best?'**
> **Mary Decker Slaney**

119

half laps of the track. It was the first time the women's 3,000 metres had been held at the Olympics. Expectation was high.

In a sense, both women were in the wrong race. It was Decker's 5,000-metres world record which Budd had bettered in South Africa. But there was no women's Olympic 5,000 metres event. Anyway, in June, the Norwegian Ingrid Kristiansen, who was running the marathon at these Games, had reset the record at 14 minutes 58.89 seconds, the first ever sub-15-minute 5,000-metre time. The world record for 3,000 metres, held by a runner from the Soviet Union which was boycotting the Games, was 8 minutes 26.78 seconds.

Budd and Decker are front runners. Not every champion is. Many prefer to hang back, letting others do the hard work of setting the pace, and near the finish line they 'kick' forward to win. Front runners are regarded as a valiant breed. They are also eminently practical: if you are at the front, you avoid the problems of getting boxed in in a race. Conversely, you never learn brusque tactics – the way to get out of a box if you find yourself in it. One of the arguments against giving Zola Budd a British passport had been that it would get her into the Olympics before she had gained the experience of racing against top runners. She might fare badly.

With this in mind, Zola Budd's coach advised her to let Decker have the lead for the first half of the race, but to keep close to Decker's shoulder. 'Let her win the first half, Zola,' he said. 'Then, you go into the lead. Win the second half of the race, that's the important part.'[2]

Mary Decker's plan was to lead the race from start to finish. She had often done it before. She and her coach did not consider Zola Budd, the new girl, a serious threat for the gold medal. The plan, if Budd did take the lead at any time before the sixth lap of the race, was to let her go.

The other women in the race, the long shots, had their eyes mainly on the silver and bronze medals. Maricica Puica, the blonde-haired Romanian who was old for a middle-distance runner – she was thirty-five – planned to stay near enough to the front to surge past the leaders near the finish and win. Puica had bloomed late, not becoming truly world class as a runner until she was twenty-nine. At thirty-three, she set a world record in the mile. Decker had since shattered it, and Maricica Puica's 1983 season had been unimpressive. Few were betting on Romania. But Wendy Sly of Britain had improved mightily since spending time in the United

States running against the best American runners. In a Decker-Budd share out she might win bronze.

Mary Decker took the lead early. According to plan she was running from the front. Just behind and beside her came Zola Budd, barefoot as usual. And there they stayed till the 1,600 metres mark, just over halfway, when, exactly as her coach had told her to, Budd began to surge forward. She could see Puica and Sly running well too, just behind Decker. For thirty to forty yards Zola Budd led the race by two or three feet, half a stride. Decker tried to regain the lead. Budd kept up. She tried again. There was no way through. Then, as they ran out of the bend into the straight with just over three laps to go, Budd, still leading, edged in to block Decker at the very moment

Mary Decker falling; behind Zola Budd are Wendy Sly and Maricica Puica

'The most famous collision since the _Titanic_ and the iceberg'

Pat Butcher, _The Times_, 1985

that she surged forward again to catch up. In the collision, Decker tripped. Her right foot raked Budd's left leg, spiking her left heel. Budd's face twisted with pain, she staggered, but kept upright. Decker screamed and began to fall. Desperate to stay upright, she tried to grab onto Zola Budd's back to regain her balance. But it was too late. Mary Decker crashed to the ground. She landed hard on her left hip, with Zola Budd's racing number in her fist.

Instinctively, Budd kept running. The crowd jeered. Later, Budd said, it felt 'like a tidal wave of concentrated hostility'. But she kept running. Zola Budd was inexperienced in international competition, but she was very experienced at being the butt of crowds. There had even been trackside demonstrations in Britain against her as a symbol of apartheid. Now, she knew she had to keep running, though she had lost her stride and other runners streamed past.

Distraught Decker with husband Richard Slaney

Decker was trying to get up. 'My first thought was I have to get up. But as soon as I made the slightest move I felt the muscle tear or pull.' She had badly injured her hip. The frustration was as painful as the injury: 'I felt I was tied to the ground. All I could do was watch them run off.' With tears of pain and anger and sorrow streaming down her cheeks, Decker was carried from the Coliseum. Maricica Puica, with her long hair streaming behind, won the race with a slow time of eight minutes, 35.96 seconds. Wendy Sly finished more than three seconds behind her to win silver. The Canadian Lynn Williams took the bronze medal. Zola Budd, her concentration broken by the collision, her foot spiked, her Games ruined, finished the race in seventh place, and was disqualified for obstruction.

She rushed over to Decker, and said, 'I'm sorry.' Still in pain, Mary Decker said, 'Get out of here! Just go.' She and Budd were both crying. Another South African Cornelia Buerki, who was running for Switzerland and had come fifth in the race, said, 'It was definitely Mary's fault.' The new Olympic champion, Maricica Puica, who had no reason to feel allegiance to either runner said, 'It was Mary's fault. She was the girl behind and should have seen the way forward.'

This was a minority opinion. 'I hold Zola responsible for what happened,' Mary Decker said bitterly. So did the crowd and ABC-TV. Decker said even more, none of it nice.

The British appealed against Zola Budd's disqualification, and Mary Peters, the former pentathlon Olympic champion, now an official on the British team, put a comforting arm around Budd's shoulder and led her out of the stadium.

The videos of the race, taken from six different angles and examined frame by frame showed that the Swiss South African Cornelia Buerki and Maricica Puica were right. Mary Decker had not been tripped; she had fallen. Budd's disqualification was lifted. ABC-TV apologized. Mary Decker did not quite. She still could not believe that she was at fault for the collision which had destroyed her Olympic hopes, but within twenty-four hours, sounding far more moderate, she tried to put the nastiness behind her. Six weeks later, her hip still sore, she said, reasonably, 'Who was at fault is irrelevant now. It was an unfortunate incident.'

But it was too late. She was nobody's sweetheart anymore.

Decker had missed the 1976 Olympics through injury; the 1980 Olympics through the boycott; and now 1984 was horrible. In 1980, the year of the boycott, Decker's frustration, her anger, had been not at losing a race, but at losing the chance to run it. Now, in 1984, her emotion and its cause were precisely the same. If she could but have run the whole race, she was sure, she would have won. Runners often fall in races; few have press conferences immediately afterwards that are shown on network television. Decker had been carried in to the press, still in tears, still in pain. It was not surprising that she had let her disappointment and her anger show. Nor was it a pretty sight. Or the best of sportsmanship or even sportspersonship. Voicing her rage was not admirable.

But it was commonplace in top-level sport. To be sure, men in sport, far more than women, have tended to behave in an ugly manner when things don't go right for them. In tennis, Nastase and Connors and MacEnroe began an era of on-court tirades. In football, more visceral punishment is dealt out.

But there is still a double standard: men are men; women can be champions but they are still supposed to be ladies. I'm not against good manners for either sex. But I think it cruel to require them in situations of extreme and unusual stress.

'My legs may be sore, my spirit may be bruised but in my heart I'm still a runner'

Zola Budd

'My legs may be sore, my spirit may be bruised, but in my heart I'm still a runner. And there are a lot more races waiting to be run,' Zola Budd said in Los Angeles. Then she too seemed to lose heart. There were death threats after the Games, and more anti-apartheid demonstrations. The weather in England was terrible, especially compared to the South African sun. Budd missed her dog Fraaier, her cat Stompie, her parents. It was said that she was considering withdrawing from athletics and going home permanently.

But she was the most visible symbol of white South Africa in the world arena. South Africa loved her, but they didn't want her to come home. The South African *Star*'s, 'We hope she chooses wisely,' meant stay to play another season.

The Budd vs. Decker 'revenge match' took place the following summer in the stadium at Crystal Palace, the British national sports centre on the outskirts of London. There was some irony in the fact that Decker could now be British too should she want to be. She had married the British discus thrower Richard Slaney.

Revenge was really no longer either runner's motivation for the race. It was – or so it seemed – money. For less than ten minutes on the track, Mary Decker Slaney, double world champion, was paid £54,000. The potentially illustrious Zola Budd was paid £90,000.

Her fee for appearing is believed to be at least four times the amount that had ever been paid to an Olympic champion for just one race. The reason Decker Slaney had been paid so much less, so the story went, was that each runner was paid what she and her advisers asked.

The appearance money, plus £36,000 for promotion and a winner's bonus of £18,000, came from television rights. The Southern Counties Amateur Athletic Association paid it out, from money they received from London Weekend Television. LWT was acting as an intermediary for Britain's ITV Sport which already held world rights to British athletics and need not have paid anything. But they paid the money to ensure that the race would take place at a time that suited TV sports programming. And British television could afford to be generous: their funds had been topped up by ABC-TV in the United States and – but of course – by South African Television.

Decker Slaney won the race. Zola Budd, who had won the appearance money stakes, finished an ignominious fourth in the race. South Africa was winning the propaganda war. The vice president of the South African Amateur Athletic Union had been attached to the Budd camp at Crystal Palace; representatives of the Republic were seen at her other races too. With such clever advisers, Zola Budd worked out a practical *modus vivendi*. She continued to race in British colours, she bought a house near London, in Surrey. But she lived for most of the year in South Africa, where in Bloemfontein a street has been named after her.

CHAPTER 10

THE PERFECT COUPLE

O lympic Village life is romantic and sexy. How could it be otherwise when a few thousand fit, nubile young athletes find themselves suddenly living in very close proximity at an emotional time – one of intensity, danger and potential glory? Passions run high. No amount of chaperoning can prevent that tension from finding an outlet.

But until very recently a lot of credence was given to that old husband's tale that abstaining from sex for a few days or a week or even for weeks before sporting competition helped one's performance, especially if one were male. Even though sporting prowess has been viewed as evidence of masculinity, sport itself has been regarded as something apart from sex, even of necessity anti-sexual. Only of late has science decided that sexual *abstinence*, if one is not accustomed to it, can be harmful to an athlete's performance.

Only one sport is seen as an embodiment of sexuality, or, anyway, of romance. This is ice skating. The roles in skating are traditional; he is larger than she, strong, capable of lifting her and whirling her around on the ice. She is responsive to his dominant touch – although it takes years of training and a lot muscle to achieve that graceful pliancy, that seemingly effortless ability to bend fluently to his will.

But the perfect pair are rarely truly the perfect couple. The greatest pair skaters ever, Irina Rodnina and her partners reigned at the Olympics throughout the 1970s, but it was she who was always the dominant member of her pair. And this is not the way of traditional romance.

There were two men in Irina Rodnina's skating life. They were the partners. She was the star. Small – four foot eleven – dark, and

Jayne Torvill and Christopher Dean

127

elegant on the ice, she was a Muskovite, born on 12 September 1949. From her father, an army officer, she inherited the ethic of coolly doing one's duty even under fire. From her mother, a local government worker, she inherited the habit of steadiness, a willingness to attend to unglamorous detail because the whole depended upon it. Her first partner, Alexei Ulanov, showed her off to advantage. With their new-look leaps and jumps, they dethroned the famous Protopopovs as world champions, and won the title three years in a row.

They would have been favourites for the 1972 Olympics at Sapporo, on the most northerly island of Japan, except that he had become involved romantically with the woman in the second-ranked pair. Her name was Ludmila Smirnova. Both couples' dancing suffered; but Rodnina's deep-edged control pulled them through and they won the Olympic title. On the victory podium she wept tears of tension. He eloped soon after with the silver medallist.

A search was made for a new partner for Rodnina. He was Alexsandr Zaitsev, tall, dark and three years her junior. Perhaps it was love, perhaps it was a way to bind him securely: they were married in 1975. They then entered the 1976 Innsbruck Olympics. Rodnina and Zaitsev won. It was her second pairs-skating gold medal.

Her third attempt at Olympic gold, in 1980, was at Lake Placid in the United States. The 1980 Winter Olympics took place amid a series of fiascos. The holes which had been drilled in the ice for flag poles were too small. A late night medal-giving ceremony for skiing, about to begin, had to be postponed because the winners had not been invited. The organization at Lake Placid, in upstate New York, left much to be desired. Even with a budget of eighty million dollars, there was a serious dearth of telephones, roads, transportation, and above all management.

Such idiocy put everyone slightly on edge. But the ice skating competition, in particular, was shaping up to be tension incarnate – a symbolic enactment of the Cold War. Irina Rodnina had taken the previous year off to have a baby. Her and Zaitsev's world title had been won by the American pair Tai Babilonia and Randy Gardner, whom the American press had named as the embattled favourites at Lake Placid. Randy Gardner was not quite over a leg injury, and the American audience was prepared to back him and his partner fiercely. During the warm-up, Gardner fell twice, and muffed a sitspin. The pair was withdrawn. Rodnina and Zaitsev won almost easily, although the crowd booed and someone shouted, 'Go Home.'

Irina Rodnina is still ranked as the most successful pair skater in the world. Thrice Olympic champion, ten times world champion (four with Ulanov, six with Zaitsev), eleven times the European champion, she skated with commanding grace.

Four minutes and twenty-eight seconds on the ice, to the music of Ravel's 'Bolero', then a crescendo of applause, and Jayne Torvill and Christopher Dean were the 1984 Olympic ice-dancing champions. The crowd at the Olympic rink in Sarajevo, Yugoslavia, applauded. This was the city where in 1914, the pistol shots which started the Great War had been fired. But for Jayne Torvill, Sarajevo, far from being the beginning of anything, was the culmination. She was twenty-six, he ten months younger. They had come a long way from the north of England.

It was a great victory. Many wanted to see more in it than there was. Even their biographer wrote: 'I asked them, the day after, if they felt closer together as a result of 'Bolero'. "Yes," they both softly answered, but Jayne ruined the romantic mood I had hoped to establish by adding with a giggle "because he's my friend, a bigger friend than he was yesterday, because he didn't fall down or anything".'[1]

Undaunted, the biographer described the 'extraordinary sexual power' of one of the moments in their Olympic 'Bolero': 'Jayne's face is cupped in Chris's hands, their lips no more than half an inch apart. Her head and arms are drawn submissively back and from top to toe she presents a sinuous curve of melting surrender.'

Perhaps you thought melting surrender had gone out with the dark ages. Not at all. And although this may not be every woman's notion of ideal sexuality, it is a precise description of the symbolism in much of ice dancing. What is projected is an antiquated view of womanhood, which like that choreographed into classical ballet seems often to verge on unintentional parody.

But whatever the symbolism of her ice dancing, Jayne Torvill was unwilling to let anyone put phony romantic words in her mouth. Shy they might call her, but in reality she was a plain-talking northerner. She had been born and reared in Nottingham, where she had learned to skate at the age of ten. Jayne Torvill was already a fairly accomplished figure skater when she began, in 1975, to skate in a pair with a local boy, Christopher Dean, on a one-

'You just can't appreciate what those medals mean to us'

Jayne Torvill

month trial. That stretched to two months and then to a decade.

Their first years were not propitious. They were limited to a maximum of six hours a week of private use of the rink, but this had to be before 6 am or after 11 pm. Jayne Torvill, who worked as an insurance clerk, used to fall asleep at her desk. Christopher Dean, a policeman, suffered from having to skate at strange but regular hours despite working irregular shifts.

But three years after they had started dancing together, they won their first national title. Even with so little practice time on the ice, in 1980 they came fourth in the world and fifth at the Olympics. Now they had an illustrious coach, Betty Calloway. Improvements in technique and artistic interpretation brought them their first European and world championships, in 1981. Torvill and Dean held on to both annual titles, with but one exception, until the 1984 Olympics. The injury which had kept them out of the 1983 Euro-peans revealed the professional intimacy of a skating pair: Dean had fallen, causing Torvill to sprain her shoulder.

Their skating had become a full-time operation. Amateurs they might be, but as early as 1979, in preparation for their first world championship, they began to receive sizeable grants. They were given £50,000 in sponsorship from the Nottingham City Council and the British Sports Aid Foundation. They were still amateurs. Olympic standards of amateurism had changed vastly. They were offered and accepted the use of a rink in Oberstdorf, West Germany, where they could skate six hours a day. This intensity is what made them champions.

They spent almost every waking hour together training. But no matter how much speculation there was, no matter how much wishful thinking by the press and the public, their private lives, such as they were, remained distinctly separate. 'I have known him so long now that he is almost a part of the furniture,' Jayne Torvill said. They saw each other nearly every waking hour, and it was not all sweetness and light. 'It is rare for us to quarrel off the ice,' she said, 'sometimes only because I am a very tolerant person.' He was full of sarcasm and argument. 'Sometimes he hurts me with his gibes, nearly always on the ice under the pressure of inventing something new,' she explained. 'Sometimes, but less often, I will be the one to lose my temper but I cannot match his brand of sarcasm.'

With the amount of training they were doing, there was very little time for a private life with anyone else. 'I doubt our partnership could survive if one or the other of us formed an attachment with somebody else off the ice.' There would be time lost, there would be jealousy, there would be diffused emotion – 'One of the secrets of our success, though it is hardly a secret, is the total commitment we make to each other on the ice.'

They were so much better than any other ice dancing pair of their time that when Torvill and Dean skated into Zetra stadium at Sarajevo, they were the out-and-out favourites for the Olympic title which they won with the highest points score ever. The following year, with no romantic illusions, they turned professional.

At Calgary in 1988, the Olympic titles were again in Soviet hands. Natalya Bestemianova and Andrey Bukin, who had been world champions for three years in a row, won the ice dance title. Gone were the days to being runners-up to Torvill and Dean.

It *was* love at first sight for two big-bicepped, thoroughly well-muscled athletes who met at the 1956 Melbourne Games. She was a discus thrower from Czechoslovakia; he a hammer thrower from the United States. The Cold War was in those days bitter; neither government thought the alliance suitable; but love triumphed. Olga Fikotova and her intended, Harold Connolly, won their respective gold medals, both setting new Olympic records. Then, she sent a special plea to the Czech leadership for permission to wed and move to the United States. When, at last, permission was grudgingly granted, Hal Connolly flew to Prague where they were married on 27 March 1957, in the most publicized sports wedding ever.

The matron of honour was the Olympic javelin champion Dana Zatopkova, and the best man was her husband the Olympic runner Emil Zatopek.

They had one unusual thing in common. Dana Ingrova and Emil Zatopek, the boy who became her husband, were born on the same day, 19 September 1922, in towns not far apart in Czechoslovakia. Marriage did not greatly hamper Dana Ingrova Zatopkova's javelin career. In 1948 she went to London for the Olympics, where she finished a modest seventh. Her husband won the 10,000 metres gold medal.

In 1952, at the Helsinki Olympics, Zatopkova and Zatopek again donned the red vests of Czechoslovakia. The Finns had built an ultra-modern stadium, and the facilities were impeccable. For once there was no political or immediate commercial cloud over the Games, although there was, outside the Olympic Stadium, a newly

'Their polished routine seemed more vulgar than sensual'

Time Magazine, of the 1988 Olympic ice dance champions

131

erected statue of the great Finnish runner Paavi Nurmi, who had been barred from the 1932 Olympics by the International Olympic Committee on the grounds of professionalism. He was still very much alive; the statue was the Finns' answer to that IOC ruling. Lest the Finns' gesture be missed, they chose fifty-five-year-old Nurmi for the honour of carrying the Olympic torch into the stadium at the opening ceremony. This unspoken insult to the IOC was an early sign that the battle against professionalism in sport would be lost.

There were sixty-nine nations at the Games. The Soviet Union was making its debut. Of the 4,925 athletes, 518 were women.

On the afternoon of the javelin final, a nervous Dana Zatopkova, whose Olympic number was 912, stood with one hand on her hip and one on the javelin, waiting to throw. She faced sixteen rivals and six rounds of throws. Her javelin soared to 50.47 metres (165 feet 7 inches) on the very first throw, her best ever and a new

**Solo sensation:
Katarina Witt,
Calgary, 1988**

Olympic record. Could it be beaten by any of the sixteen? Every moment of the competition was anxious, but the only one that was dangerous came in the last round, when the Russian Alexandra Chudina's javelin took flight. Zatopkova held her breath, the judges ran to check the distance, and it was within two feet of Dana Zatopkova's throw, but Zatopkova had won.

Her husband was watching in the stadium, and the crowd began to cheer. Not just because she had set an Olympic record. Not even because no Czech woman had ever before won a gold medal in track and field athletics at the Olympics. But because her husband, the track star of the Games, had also won gold at those Olympics, in the 10,000 metres and – on the very day of her victory – in the 5,000 metres. No other married couple had ever won gold medals in track and field athletics at the same Olympics. A few days later, he also won the marathon. Zatopkova and Zatopek became the toast of Helsinki.

Two years later in Brussels Zatopkova and Zatopek did it again at the European championships. She won the javelin championship; he the 10,000 metres.

She was now the oldest woman ever to break a world record. She was thirty-five years 255 days old on 1 June 1958, when she threw 56.73 metres in a stadium in Prague. The record she broke by well over a metre had stood four years; but Zatopkova's new record was to stand only fifty-three days.

She continued to compete after her husband's retirement. In 1960, when Dana Zatopkova was thirty-seven years 248 days old, she won a silver medal at the Rome Olympics, becoming the oldest woman ever to win an Olympic athletics medal.

The only person who had been at all able to comfort her fiancé after his Olympic defeat in the 400 metres race was Ann Packer. There were tears brimming in Robbie Brightwell's eyes. The captain of the British athletics team at the 1964 Tokyo Games had expected to win but he had come only fourth. He seemed inconsolable. Packer's own hopes at these Games had been disappointed too. She had been touted for gold but had won only silver in her event, also the 400 metres. Now what they both needed was something to celebrate. If she were to win another medal, she felt sure, he would feel better.

The women's 800-metres final was the next day, and before his shattering defeat, Ann Packer had even been considering with-

Something to celebrate: Robbie Brightwell and Ann Packer

drawing. She had only run the event twice in her life before the Olympics, and had finished an unpromising fifth in her heat, and only third in her semi-final. Besides that, the skinny, twenty-two-year-old schoolteacher knew she was physically and mentally tired.

But now she had a new motivation. She would try to win the gold medal for him. And the field was wide open because the official world record holder, the Australian Dixie Willis, had had an attack of nerves and failed to make the final. An even faster 800-metres runner, Sin Kim Dan, of North Korea, had been barred from the Olympics because she took part in the unsanctioned Games of the New Emerging Forces in Djakarta. There, on 12 November 1963, she had broken the two-minute barrier with a 1-minute 59.1-second run. But it was not officially recognized. (See pp. 17–18.)

In the Olympic final, the favourite Maryvonne Dupureur of France was in decidedly good form. And the New Zealander Marise Chamberlain was fast too.

At the starter's gun, Dupureur rushed into the lead, leaving Ann Packer trailing toward the back of the field. Dupureur led for the first lap in a fast time of 58.9 seconds. Packer, noticing the time on the scoreboard, was heartened: 'It had not seemed so fast.'

When Chamberlain, who was in front of Packer, made no move to catch Dupureur, Ann Packer moved into an outside lane to get clear of the pack and put on the pressure. Having been seventh, she passed Dupureur and didn't slow down, finishing five yards and 0.8 seconds ahead of her in an unexpected new world record time of 2 minutes 1.1 seconds. At the finish, a gladdened Robbie Brightwell was there to greet her.

'The whole story sounds like one of those romantic serials in a woman's magazine. But this one happens to be true,'[2] the British sportswriter Christopher Brasher, a former Olympic athlete, wrote in his fascinating *Tokyo 1964 Diary*. The story is, in fact, a reversal of what happens in those romantic serials. But he is right, it is romantic, and it does happen to be true.

A legend in her own time: Grete Waitz

CHAPTER 11

THE FURTHEST RACE

*T*he nightmare she has goes like this: she is lost in a department store, crashing through racks of clothing, rushing up and down escalators, trying to get out. The race is starting without her. 'I hear the gun go off and I run in circles. Finally I escape and join the pack. I have to run wildly to catch up with the leaders.'[1]

Then Joan Benoit wakes up. It is a classic anxiety dream. She often has it before an important race.

For most of the California night before the first-ever women's Olympic marathon in August 1984, Joan Benoit lay wide awake in her bed, unable to sleep. To make the time pass, she listened over and over on her Walkman to the theme music from *Chariots of Fire*. When at last she fell asleep, Joan Benoit had that familiar, frightening dream.

In the morning, if her knee held out, the dark-haired American from Maine would run the Olympic marathon, 26 miles 385 yards in the gathering heat and smog – past the Pacific ocean beaches, down city streets, down the cordoned middle of the Marine Free-way, crossing the finish line – if she made it – in the crowded Los Angeles Coliseum.

Only the year before, five-foot two-and-a-quarter-inch tall Benoit, a college coach, had run the fastest ever women's marathon. In the Olympic year of 1984, no one anywhere bettered her 2-hour 22.43 minute time, not even the great Grete Waitz, the skinny, fair-haired Norwegian ex-school-teacher who was the most famous, most respected marathoner in the world. A string of victories in the New York marathon had made Waitz the first female international marathon star. It was Grete Waitz's world best time which Benoit had bettered.

Because the marathon is run on roads and streets instead of on a track, the courses vary – some have more hills, some more twists and turns, some have cobblestones. There are races for both sexes, and for women only. It may be that women run faster in a race where the top men, who at present are faster than the fastest women, set the pace. For these reasons, only world best performances, not world records are recognized officially in the marathon. But it is not a distinction that is rigidly adhered to in discussing the event. Waitz's world best time had been set in the London marathon; Benoit had bettered it in the Boston. In both events, there were men running.

Since Benoit's achievement, Waitz had struck back in another way. She was now world champion. Waitz always shone best on great occasions, and was verging on thirty – old enough for peak endurance and experienced enough to be race-smart. And Waitz was five inches taller than Benoit – most of it leg.

Even so, if Joan Benoit was in good working order, she knew she had a good chance of beating Grete Waitz in the race. But was she? Would Benoit's rickety right knee that was only twenty-seven years old but behaved like ninety, last the race?

On an ordinary training run in March, the knee, an important instrument of her trade, had failed her. It was as though suddenly a tiny spring in the knee popped out of place and resettled in the wrong position. Something mechanical, she sensed, was obstructing the joint's natural movement. She hobbled home. The injury kept nagging her. At her doctor's instruction, she took time off to ease it. During the periods she couldn't run, she kept up her fitness with intense bursts on an exercise bike.

Five weeks before the 12 May Olympic trials, on another little run, the knee locked. On the way home that time, it was painful even to lift her right leg over a twig. She had to step down with the left leg every time she came to a kerb. and then gingerly drag along the right.

Cortisone, rest, nothing helped; her knee hurt or locked when she ran. And the Olympic trials were looming. Even though she was, on paper, the fastest woman in the world at the marathon distance, to gain entry to the Olympics, Joan Benoit had to place in the trials.

Just two weeks before the Olympic trials, Benoit underwent a knee operation in Eugene, Oregon, the runners' town, where she had gone to train. The surgery was a desperate last resort.

She checked into the Oregon hospital. They gave her the anaesthetic, and then the doctor probed her knee with an arthroscope until he found and removed the lump called a plica, which had lodged against a tendon and was interfering with the movement of her knee. So far so good. She would recover from the surgical wound and the lost training and fitness. But would she recover soon enough?

To complicate matters, since she was favouring the sore knee whenever she did run in training, she damaged a hamstring on the other leg. The consensus (and even Benoit shared it) was that it would take a miracle for her to run well enough long enough so soon after surgery to place in the marathon in the Olympic trial.

On Easter Sunday, Joan Benoit went to Mass and asked God why he had sent this injury to her at this time. 'Why me? Why now?' Then she looked across the church and saw Alberto Salazar, who held the men's world marathon record. She felt jealous of his health. 'Then, when my envy passed, I reconfirmed what I'd always believed: that God has a reason for everything he does. The whole situation was in His hands, not mine. I prayed then that if I couldn't run in the trials and Olympics, God would grant Alberto the two best races of his life.'

Came the day of the Olympic trials. She needed third place or better to get into the Olympics. 'Miraculously, my legs held up.' Benoit's fragile legs not only lasted the distance, they carried her to victory. 'I ran what I still consider the race of my life that day.'

But the race that counts in the record books, the first ever Olympic marathon, was still to be run. It was not at all clear that the knee would take the strain again. And the Olympic field was fast – not just the best runners in the United States; the best in the world.

You need to sleep well and eat well before a marathon. The nightmare was the only proof Benoit had that she had slept at all. She hadn't really eaten either – she was suffering from nervous stomach, nausea, diarrhoea, the works. Things didn't look good.

It was no consolation either to know that elsewhere in Los Angeles, Grete Waitz was also having problems with her stomach. Everyone in running knew about Grete Waitz's perennial 'runner's stomach'. It didn't curtail her triumph. The three in a row in world best time in New York had been won despite cramps and diarrhoea, so had the London marathon, and in Helsinki, the world championship. Many thought Waitz was the likely winner of the first Olympic marathon – if it wasn't Benoit or the other hollow-cheeked Norwegian, Ingrid Kristiansen, the new 5,000-metres world record

> **'When I first started running I was so embarrassed I'd walk when cars passed me. I'd pretend I was looking at the flowers'**
>
> Joan Benoit

holder and a rising star. She would become the greatest distance runner of her generation, but she hadn't made an indelible mark yet. The woman most likely to succeed if the day was hot was the Portuguese European champion Rosa Mota.

The sparrowlike Edith Piaf of the marathon, Rosa Mota, smoothed her cropped black hair with her fingers and stood behind the startline first on one foot, then on the other, waiting for the race to begin. Five-foot two-inch tall Rosa Mota was just a quarter of an inch shorter than Benoit and two and a half pounds lighter. She was fourteen months younger than Benoit and looked years older. On this damp, dull, cool California morning, 5 August 1984, the sky was grey with early morning fog. As the clock ticked forward to the 8 am start of the first Olympic women's marathon, Rosa Mota silently willed the weather to turn hot.

The heat reminded her of home. Home for Mota was an apartment near the ocean in sunny Foz do Douro, in wine country on the outskirts of Oporto, Portugal's second largest city.

The heat reminded her of her first marathon too, which she had run reluctantly on a sweltering day in Athens, in the European championships of 1982. That day the marathon was twice as far as Rosa Mota had ever run, even in training. She won. She had found her event. That championship was the first women's marathon in international competition. It was held in the very stadium where the first (all-male) marathon of the modern Olympics had taken place in 1896. How sweet it would be to win on another historic occasion.

As the morning fog began to burn off, Rosa Mota smiled. The day was going to be blazing hot.

Grete Waitz's brow furrowed. She was leery of the heat. She and Ingrid Kristiansen had stayed home to train in the relative cool of Norway until just before the Games. Now, as Waitz pinned up her braids so they would not smack her in the face as she ran, she was wondering if that had been a mistake.

But even if the weather did slow her down, she still had the advantage of a tremendous ability to kick, to speed up toward the end of a race, even a marathon, when the others were usually flagging. No one could match Waitz's amazing fast finish. That often was the decisive factor in the race.

She intended to run a tactical race. Staying with the pack, but somewhere near the front, she would go at a modest pace for twenty

'If Grete had been there it would have meant a little more'

Rosa Mota's coach, following her world championship victory, 1987 miles. Then she would kick the pace up, finishing with a finale of speed. Grete Waitz had it in her to kick over the last 10,000 metres, to cap twenty gruelling miles of running with a fast six-mile spurt. But the August sun would be high during the last six miles, the sea breezes would have been left behind. It would be hot. But of course it would be hot for everyone.

Now the adrenaline was beginning to flow. The fifty women who were entered in the race took their warmups off, and pinned or

Rosa Mota, number 475, at the 1987 world championships in Rome. She eventually won by a mile

taped their running numbers on. Pinned numbers chafed Joan Benoit. Absentmindedly she checked with her fingers that her number was taped firmly in place. Maine had been humid and hot all summer. Benoit would be just fine in the heat. If the knee lasted.

To win, she would have to take the lead early, before the pace hotted up and then, if she was far enough ahead, hope that she could maintain that pace to the finish line. She had no kick, no ability to burst into speed at the end of a race. Stamina and a fastish, controlled, even pace were her characteristic running weapons. In June and much of July, she had polished those weapons with ever faster weekly twenty-mile runs in heat-struck Maine.

Moments before the start, she put on a white cotton painter's cap. It would keep the dark hair fringing her forehead from bouncing. A cap was also good to wear in the heat. She wore it back to front.

The race began at a cautious pace. Benoit's stomach was still bothering her. There was some medication in a plastic bag attached to the inside of her shorts. But with the ABC television cameras rolling, she didn't dare reach into her shorts. For the first three miles, she ran with the pack. But she felt hemmed in. As the women jockeyed for position, Benoit had to break her stride. It happened again. The only way to get out of that crush was to get to the front, where she could run at her own rhythm. And if that meant taking on the work of leading the race, she would do it, because her only chance was to run her own race. She had just taken the lead when she arrived at the first water stop. The thought of getting back in that crowd was enough. She skipped the water. As most of the others stopped, Joan Benoit pulled further away. She was still worried that the knee would pack up; she knew she had to take it easy, but she was taking it easy and leading the pack by twenty yards. She glanced over her shoulder. No one was making any effort to catch her. That was worrying. 'I thought, this is the Olympic marathon, and you're going to look like a showboat leading for halfway and then having everyone pass you.' The sensible thing was to slow down. But the 5-minute-40-second-a-mile pace, not especially fast for the distance, felt right.

At five miles she led by thirteen seconds. The leaders of the pack were Waitz, Rosa Mota, whose every marathon was getting faster, and Ingrid Kristiansen, whose best marathon time on record was far better than Mota's. With them was Priscilla Welch, the Briton whose career was beginning at age thirty-nine. Welch had slipped off her wedding ring and watch to lighten her load.

The gap widened. The pack of women runners and the male TV commentators were certain that Benoit was going too fast too soon. Her pace had quickened to 5 minutes 20 seconds a mile. Her slightly splayed stride, seen head-on by the camera, looked awkward. Was knee trouble making it so? the commentators wondered. Waitz and Kristiansen and Mota still made no move to catch her. Like the TV men, they thought, 'Benoit will break down, and we'll take her.'

At nineteen miles, Benoit's lead was a full two minutes. It was 80 degrees Fahrenheit. Hot. And the smog was at full choke. It was almost two hours into the race, and Benoit, her shirt drenched with sweat, was tuned to her own steady rhythm, apparently thinking her own calm thoughts. 'I just was praying that my knee would not give way', she said later.

Suddenly, Rosa Mota, who had been waiting for Waitz to make a move, and who feared Benoit was becoming uncatchable, strode ahead of the two Norwegians and the rest of the pack. 'I felt good, and I decided to attack.' Immediately, and only a little ahead of her planned race schedule, Grete Waitz switched on the speed. It was high time too, Benoit was nearly out of sight.

Kristiansen and Mota went with Waitz, but they couldn't catch her. They stayed as near as they could. They were going for the bronze medal now.

Benoit, way ahead, kept on running at her own seemingly nerveless pace. But Grete Waitz was closing the gap. Second by second, as they neared the Olympic stadium, where they would run the final lap, Waitz, her wan face showing the strain, was getting closer.

In the Los Angeles Coliseum, for nearly two and a half hours, 77,000 people had been watching the marathon on the huge stadium television. As they and the TV commentators watched the frontrunner Joan Benoit's solitary run they had hoped against hope, but doubted, that her knee would last the distance. Then, as they began to expect, to hope for, to count on a Benoit victory, Waitz surged forward, and the crowd which was yearning for Joan Benoit's victory realized it was suddenly in doubt.

The marathon had been a procession; now they were watching a race. Moment by moment, Waitz was gaining on the leader. And just behind Grete Waitz, Ingrid Kristiansen and Rosa Mota were having their own duel in the sun for the Olympic bronze medal.

As Joan Benoit ran through the tunnel that led into the stadium, she could hear the crowd cheering. She was almost there, and Grete Waitz was still behind her. One thought flashed through Joan

Benoit's mind: 'Once you leave this tunnel your life will be changed forever.' Then she came out into the sunlight. The crowd gave an exultant roar. Benoit's legs went wobbly with emotion. Now she began to run the last lap, on the stadium track. As she lapped the Coliseum, Joan Benoit raised her arm high and waved her white cap in the air.

Grete Waitz was entering the tunnel, moving fast. She had sliced an impressive thirty seconds off Benoit's lead. But she and everyone else now knew that she had left it too late. 'I could perhaps have run faster,' Waitz said, 'but because of that heat, I was afraid of dying.'

As the runners rushed, one by one, into the stadium for the final lap of the longest race, the crowd gave each one of them an emotional roar of welcome.

To her own surprise, the European Champion, Rosa Mota finished third in a time four minutes faster than she had ever run before. Perhaps Ingrid Kristiansen, who was better on paper, had run too many miles that season, or maybe it was the heat. 'I didn't think I could get a medal,' Rosa Mota said. 'But I'm glad I didn't try to go with Joan because I don't think I would have finished.'

An elated Priscilla Welch finished in sixth place, setting a new British record.

To have run in the first women's Olympic marathon was an enormous achievement. Emotions ran high. None more than Joan Benoit's, 'I was so charged up that when I broke the tape, I could have turned around and run another twenty-six miles, though maybe not in a time of 2:24:52, a minute and a half ahead of Grete Waitz,' she said.

Now something a little strange happened. Although the media gave huge coverage to Benoit's important victory, they gave nearly as much space to the terrible personal battle of Gabriela Andersen-Schiess, who toward the end of the race, pushed herself onward even after, in runner's parlance, she had 'hit the wall'. Her alarming entrance into the Coliseum, bent double, limping, her body's stores of energy and fluid depleted, was beamed around the world. Gabriela Andersen-Schiess fought an heroic struggle against the limits of her own body and finished in thirty-seventh position. But press coverage was turning her into an emblem of female frailty.

Their concentration on the 'weaker sex angle' had resulted, in 1928, in the two-and-a-half-minute 800 metres being plucked from

Historic victory: Joan Benoit, winning in Los Angeles, 1984

the Olympic roster (see Chapter 1, Elbowing In, page 8), not to return until 1960. Longer distances for women at the Games had ever after been resisted.

That story is known to most female runners. In Los Angeles, in 1984, they just were not having that. Benoit, Waitz and the others reiterated what the doctors had said: Andersen-Schiess would be fully recovered in a day or two, even though she had run without proper conditioning in dire circumstances – smog, heat, the fastest opponents in the world.

In fact, because of some characteristics of the female metabolism, women tend to feel more comfortable than men in the final stages of a marathon. Many people, considering women and men of comparable running standard, have noticed that women less often come up against marathoners' wall. Because women sweat less, they become less dehydrated. It has been hypothesized that their additional fat stores mean that their reserve energy lasts longer. This latter point is now in some doubt. But it certainly can be argued that women (who hold most of the ultra-distance records in track and swimming) are better suited than men to running long distances. These, of course, are the very races that for so many decades women have been 'protected' from running.

The winner of the first women's Olympic marathon, Joan Benoit, was no radical, no ideologue, but she understood the important implications of her achievement. 'This win is a triumph for women's athletics,' Benoit told the TV cameramen, the reporters and the newspaper photographers who gathered around her. 'Now that we have proved that we can stand the conditions of the marathon, maybe they will include the 10,000 metres in the Olympics in the future.' A great deal of pressure had been brought to bear to get the marathon into the 1984 Olympics; now the women's running movement readjusted its aim. It was soon announced that the 10,000 metres race would be run at the 1988 Seoul Olympics. Women had won another victory. Was it because of their concerted effort, or was it the magic of Benoit's euphoric triumph, which had been seen by millions of people worldwide, and which had captured many of their imaginations?

It is said that a Greek woman named Melpomene – her name is the same as that of the Muse of Tragedy – wanted, in 1896, to run in the first Olympic marathon. Her entry refused, she ran anyway, alone, starting well behind the men and finishing in about four and a half hours. She ran her final lap around the outside of the stadium. She is a kind of modern Atalanta, a figure of legend in the history of the marathon.

Over the eighty-eight years that would elapse until Joan Benoit's victory, the women's marathon grew stealthily. The gloom and loneliness of women's early marathon history is hard to imagine in an era when women running marathons are shown live on satellite television.

Women not only had to fight to endure the marathon distance, they had to fight off officials who wanted to bar them from the competition 'for their own good'. Those few women who ran, did it 'unofficially', running in unsanctioned record attempts, or in men's races.

The records are sketchy. What is known is this: in 1918, a woman finished thirty-eighth in a French marathon. In 1923, a woman finished the South African Comrades Marathon. On 3 October, 1926, three decades after the rebirth of the Games, Violet Piercy ran the first recorded women's marathon, in 3 hours 40 minutes 22 seconds, over a course which meandered through the London suburb of Chiswick.

But with little encouragement and much discouragement, so few women ran the marathon that it took nearly forty years to better that world best time. That honour is variously ascribed to the American Mary Lepper who is said to have shaved the record of more than three minutes in 1963, and to the Briton Dale Greig, who sliced Piercy's time by thirteen minutes a year later.

In 1966, Roberta Louise Gibb rode four days and four nights on a Greyhound bus from San Diego to run, she hoped, in the famous, prestigious, men-only Boston marathon. Her mother, who lived in Massachusetts, drove her to the start. Gibb then hid in the bushes near the startline. When about half of the male marathoners had passed her hiding place, she jumped out and joined the race. No one noticed her – they must have been deadly serious types as she was running in a black leotard and a beret. Or maybe they ignored her deliberately because they thought she had the right to run. She finished the race in under three and a half hours, becoming the first woman ever to run the Boston. That night the race manager, Will Cloney said, 'What girl? I know of no woman who ran. Our rules do not permit women to run.'[2]

The following year, Katherine Switzer got an official entry by applying as K. Switzer. When officials spotted her, one of them attempted to grab the number, but Switzer's boyfriend threw a bodyblock. The next day the Boston marathon got more publicity than it had ever received before.

But it was not until 1972, seventy-five years after the first Boston marathon, that women were admitted on the same conditions as men. For the first time, says Joe Falls, the historian of the Boston, 'On March 28, 1972, the women of the world were looked upon as first class citizens by the Boston Athletic Association. It was a mere fifty-two years after they had been accorded the right to vote.' This milestone in women's distance running encouraged the women's running movement to lobby for the Olympic marathon.

By now the marathon boom was on. Women were eager to run road races as official entrants instead of as bandits. Even though then – as now – when compared to men, few women were as yet running the marathon, and they were training less than men and in an amateurish and haphazard manner, large chunks began to be hacked off the women's world best time. The quest was on for the three hour marathon. On 31 August 1971, the Australian Adrienne Beames crashed through that psychological barrier, with a run of 2 hours 46 minutes 30 seconds.

Forty women from seven countries competed in the first Women's International Marathon, which was held in October 1974 in Waldniel, Germany. Two years later there were forty-five finishers from nine countries.

Now Grete Waitz began to get in on the act. In a way, she turned to the marathon because it was *not* an Olympic event. She had shattered the world 3,000 metres record twice, in 1975 and 1976. But at the 1978 European championships, though she was in peak form, two East European runners didn't just pass her at the finish, they whizzed by. Waitz and her husband-coach were devastated: they suspected the others were using anabolic steroids.

The marathon was still low key, and as it was not an Olympic event, it was less likely that there would be drug abuses. Waitz also decided to compete in her first marathon, the 1978 New York, because she suspected her talent was for long distances, and because she and her husband were given free plane tickets by the organizers, and wanted to see New York. Her 1978 victory in the New York marathon, possibly then the largest and certainly the most hyped marathon in the world, was the first of a string of wins there in world record time that would make her world famous.

The rise of the marathon was the sport story of the decade. What had been a rare event for both sexes, was becoming almost a commonplace. But despite the increase in numbers, not a millisecond was pared from the men's marathon in the decade of the 1970s. It was stuck at 2:08:33.6 for a dozen years, until in 1981 it went down by 15 seconds. The women's marathon was where the action was. The record was sliced ten times, and whittled down by more than half an hour. Men were running hard, as hard as ever. Women were running for the first time. The men had come close to their fastest potential speed; the women were only getting started.

By 1980, the United States alone had eighty thousand female marathoners – and 190 of them were capable of running the distance in under three hours. By 1982 that number had grown to 265. Yet running the marathon was still odd for a woman – a world record breaker and the Olympic marathon champion Joan Benoit would later admit that in the early days, she had felt funny: 'When I first started running I was so embarrassed I'd walk when cars passed me. I'd pretend I was looking at the flowers.'[3]

In 1983, Benoit ran a world best in none other than the Boston marathon. That was the race that made her the 1984 Olympic favourite until her knee locked.

After Joan Benoit entered the Los Angeles Coliseum victorious, her life *was* changed forever. There would be no more scrimping. That year alone, she earned $402,000. There would be no semblance of anonymity either. Now she was as famous as Grete the Great. She made appearances, she wrote a book, she was American marathoning's foremost star.

As she had planned to do, win or lose, she marched into church to the tune of *Chariots of Fire*, and got married to the man she had been going out with for some time, Scott Samuelson. There were more injuries, more victories, and in the winter of 1987, her first baby. (See the last pages of Chapter 4, Mothers Run Best.) Now that she had won the Olympic gold medal, Joan Benoit had another goal: to break the next barrier, to run a marathon in less than two hours twenty minutes.

But Ingrid Kristiansen, not Joan Benoit, was now regarded as the distance runner of the era, and had been at least since 21 April 1985. Joan Benoit got the news the next day, when she went to the post office to pick up her mail, and the Maine postman told her that Ingrid Kristiansen had run a new world marathon best of 2 hours 21:06 minutes in London.

The 'other Norwegian', who had lived for so long in Grete Waitz's shadow, has achieved unprecedented eminence. She is the only athlete of either sex ever to hold the 5,000 metres, 10,000 metres and marathon world records simultaneously. Amazingly, she also holds the half-marathon and the 15,000 metres world records.

Whittling world records is a different art from winning races. To win a race you go as slowly as possible – only as fast as is comfortable and necessary to get ahead of the pack. You run your own race if possible, and at a 'safe' distance, so that if you don't come first, you do finish second or third. To break a world record you have to go at a faster pace than you are sure you can keep up.

'If you go for a record,' Ingrid Kristiansen says, 'you can break down and maybe finish fifth or sixth.' To a champion, finishing down in the field can be embarrassing. Better, many say, not to tempt fate.

Some champion marathoners just aren't interested in shattering records. 'Unlike Ingrid,' says Rosa Mota, speaking of herself and her coach, 'we never think about world records. The big competitions always come first. It is more important to win a medal than to break a world record.'

In Rome, in 1987, Rosa Mota won the world marathon championship in the scorching September sun. It was a great victory, diminished slightly by the fact that because of injury or other commitments, neither Kristiansen nor Waitz nor Joan Benoit was there. Many people agree with Rosa Mota that because of the nature of the marathon, the world record doesn't prove anything: 'Marathons are always on different courses and in variable conditions, so times are not important,' she says. 'In Boston for example, you get front wind.' (Is that a dig at Joan Benoit?)

Ingrid Kristiansen cares deeply about being the best in the world. She believes fear of failure is what keeps many of the others from attempting it. 'I think Grete is afraid to run as fast as she must to break 2:20,' Kristiansen says, perhaps partly to egg Grete Waitz on. 'If she tried I think she could do it. She wants to *win* races' – not risk losing them badly.

And the race of races is the Olympic marathon. It looked as if Ingrid Kristiansen would be the one to beat in the 1988 Olympic marathon. Then, the geniuses who construct Olympic timetables made it impossible for women (but not men) to compete in the 1988 Olympics over both the new 10,000 metre and the marathon distances. Not long before Christmas 1987, Ingrid Kristiansen, who

Ingrid Kristiansen sets new world 10,000 metres record in Norway, 1986

was world champion at 10,000 metres, announced that she had chosen the shorter distance – she wanted to become the first Olympic champion at 10,000 metres.

Grete Waitz may have regarded that decision as a Christmas present. Certainly it was welcomed by Benoit and by Rosa Mota, who would arrive at the Olympics as world champion. At the time of this writing, the start of the 1988 track season, one of The Four – Benoit, Kristiansen, Mota and Waitz – is thought likely to break the 2 hour 20-minute barrier soon.

The odds are on Ingrid Kristiansen. But Joan Benoit is undaunted. 'The woman who breaks it will undoubtedly usher in a new age in the sport of running, the way Roger Bannister did when he shattered the four-minute mile,' she wrote in her autobiography, *Running Tide*. 'My desire to make this watershed is akin to the adventurer's need to explore unknown ground. Whether or not I achieve this goal, I have to try.'

OLYMPIC EYE: A SPORTWATCHER'S GUIDE

ARGUING POINTS: THE ISSUES AT A GLANCE

Are men better than women at sport?

*E*ven though women have beaten men in the open events at the Olympics (see page 10), and there is evidence that women are as good as men at many sports and better at some, this is a phoney issue, largely for three reasons.

Fewer women than men are involved in sport. If the same numbers of women as men were involved in sport, there would be a larger pool of athletes and therefore a higher standard. Even today, there may be a woman in Edinburgh or Edmonton or Evanston who could be an Olympic champion but dares not engage seriously in what she has been taught is a masculine pursuit. Instead, she engages in such delicate, typically feminine tasks as scrubbing floors, milking cows, carrying toddlers (and if she is a nurse, carrying adults).

Few of the women who are involved in sport dare take it as seriously as men do. Except at the very top, women train less than their male counterparts. A number of studies have shown that because women have less leisure time than men and because of the other counter-pressures (fears of getting sweaty, getting muscles, training yourself into a man, being called unfeminine), women who do quite well in a marathon, for example, will have trained fewer hours at a relatively less intense pace than men of the same comparable standard.

Finally, if all sports were organized the way boxing, judo and weightlifting are, more women would beat more men sooner. In these three sports, conventionally the most macho, the athletes compete in weight categories. The average woman weighs less and is shorter than the average man. If women competed against men of comparable weight, we would have many more who would equal or surpass men. To be sure there are differences in muscle mass and fibre and so forth between the sexes, but the shapes and sizes of men and women vary tremendously, and brawny women would come into their own.

Potentially women make better jockeys than men but prejudice keeps women's numbers severely limited. Results in other equestrian sports show they ride as well as men, perhaps better, and they have less trouble making the weight. Because of the way their bodies function, they *may* also be better at the super-long distance ultra-events and at the marathon (see page 146), although the latter may not be long enough to show women to full advantage. This superiority at ultra-distances may turn out to be a myth. But women make better divers, partly because they have more fat insulation. And because of their lower centre of balance, flexibility and strong lower bodies (relative to their upper bodies) they are more suited than men to the sport of weightlifting.

Even though women were barred from top-level equestrian sport until fairly recently, they dominate the world championships and may soon dominate the Olympics. The winning Olympic teams tend to include a high percentage of women. Equestrianism requires of the rider tremendous fitness, balance, timing – and strength and courage.

If girls and women were encouraged as much as boys and men are to engage in sport, if they were equally encouraged to get serious about it, and given the same support – funding, prizes, facilities, acclaim – more women would play more sports better, and even more than already have done so would surpass men. The important point is that women should get equal opportunity at an equal number of sports.

Is sport dangerous for women?
No, it is dangerous for men.

In any contact sport, like Olympic running (all that elbowing), boxing, basketball, hockey and wrestling, and even in noncontact sports, the penis is a sitting duck. The protective box or jock strap sells well. (An aluminium sports bra never sold because it was not needed.) Even a racing bicycle can do injury to the male genitals. Bikes with dropped handle bars bring the rider's legs close to the stomach, and the testicles can get squashed or twisted against the saddle. This can lead to gangrene and amputation. Such cases have been reported in the medical journal, the *Lancet.*

Not only that. Because the average man is heavier than the average woman, and has more bone and muscle mass, he is a more dangerous missile. So, if two men run into each other on the hockey field or the track, there is apt to be more injury than if two women do.

For these two reasons, a case could be made for banning men from contact sports (in practice, from all Olympic sports) and from bicycling. But since sport does provide a healthy outlet for the hardy and for the spectator, women, being sturdier and less vulnerable to injury than men, should be encouraged to play these sports.

For heavensakes, isn't there some danger to women?
Less than to men, but yes some.

Although for generations women were warned of the perils of sport, there seems to be only one specifically female danger. Top champions often take time off to have babies (see Chapter 4, Mothers Run Best). But while they are training at the intensity that wins Olympic medals many women stop having menstrual periods. Their periods usually resume when training lessens.

The big danger, however, is calcium loss when they are not having any periods. The levels of oestrogen in their bodies is lowered, and like women who have passed the menopause, they lose calcium, which leads to loss of bone mass and can make them prone to fractures. This can be combated with calcium and hormonal therapy. One recent study suggests that in some cases fertility can be lessened.

There appears to be no specific danger to sportswomen who are training at recreational level, only to those women who train with enough intensity to get to the very top. The fact is that Olympic and professional sport in modern times requires so much training, so much over-use of an athlete's limbs, that athletes of both sexes are frequently injured.

Olympic gymnasts of either sex may practise the same routine twenty, even thirty thousand times, each time their hands and wrists or ankles and legs taking the impact. Runners often stress their hamstrings, Achilles tendons, shins, you name it. Mary

Decker Slaney and Joan Benoit Samuelson have even required surgery (see Chapter 9, Collision Course and Chapter 11, The Furthest Race) but so have their male counterparts.

Why do world records keep improving?

Every season, women run faster, jump higher and throw further. Why? There are several reasons. Sports champions of both sexes, and women especially, take sport more seriously today than they did years ago, so they train harder and longer. Most Olympic contenders in the East and in the West train full-time.

Now, too, sophisticated, legitimate sports science is used to analyse the best way to tackle each sport. Illegitimate methods are sometimes used too.

Physiologists and coaches are telling athletes the best ways to train for their particular sport. Weight-training, for example, is commonplace in most sports.

Nutritionists are learning what is the best food to eat. Physiologists and coaches are analysing the techniques you need for each event and helping their athletes to learn the most efficient ones.

Engineers are designing better clothing and equipment too. Racing swimsuits are minimal and have less drag than they once did. Shoes in all sports provide more spring and speed and support than ever before. Because of electronic timing records can now be noted in milliseconds.

Some of the new records were achieved with illegal drugs (see below).

Another reason for the increase in records is that people are just getting bigger. Longer legs can help in the jumps, and a bigger frame which may naturally hold more muscle helps in throwing and skiing, for example.

Because more people now engage in sport, there is a larger pool from which to choose champions. In other words, competition is stiffer in all sports, and particularly in women's sport. Because this is so, the standards go up, and world records continue to improve.

Drug abuse

To build muscle fast and thereby increase strength, some top athletes of both sexes take drugs. Men are by far the worst drug abusers. But women get the worst press on this issue.

Anabolic steroids, the drugs which have been most talked about, are synthetic versions of the male hormone testosterone. Steroids increase weight and muscle bulk, and therefore strength, quickly.

Athletes who take them in huge doses can train harder, more often and in longer sessions than they might otherwise. It is primarily for this reason that steroids build muscle, and probably strength, fast. Anabolic steroids are not magical potions which will turn a human sloth into a champion.

Another increasingly abused drug is human growth hormone, which helps athletes grow big. Human growth hormone, also known as somatotrophin, a scarce and expensive drug, was designed to combat dwarfism in children. It elongates the long bones. A number of male athletes have admitted taking it. It is not banned because there is no test for it. Human growth hormone may cause bone damage and gigantism and may have other dangerous side effects. Hospital thefts have deprived children who need the drug of treatment.

Anabolic steroids taken in the enormous doses athletes use have dangerous side-effects, including cancer and severe liver damage, aggressive 'roid rages', severe acne, facial hair and voice deepening in women, and impotence and breasts in men.

It is estimated that up to 1.3 million people take anabolic steroids, human growth hormone and other strength and size-enhancing drugs. This total includes about a million Americans and 300,000 Britons and Western and Eastern Europeans.

Few of these drug abusers are female because there are so many fewer women in sport than there are men, and because traditional notions of femininity deter many women from getting bulky or big.

Only 1,896 women competed at the summer and winter Olympics of 1984, compared to 6,460 men. It is likely that a good number of these women at the top level of sport, and some who are preparing for the Olympics and for other major competitions, did and do take the drugs. But the average recreational sportswoman, the club and even the county player, would not consider taking them. These women want to avoid big muscles because of the stigma still attached to muscular women in conventional society.

But the male player typically wants as many muscles as he can get. Muscles enhance his masculine image. When he is offered the drugs in the gym or by doctor or coach – these are the three main sources – he is less likely to say no.

And just as men can build muscles without drugs, so can women. 'There is no physiological reason to assume that the only way for a woman to become muscular is by abusing male hormones; hard training alone can do it,' is a point that is rightly stressed by the research scientists Tom Donohoe and Neil Johnson in their book *Foul Play: Drug Abuse in Sport*.

Amphetamines, known as uppers, are used in some sports; calming Beta-blockers in others.

Blood-doping is a method in which an athlete is reinjected with up to two pints of her own blood shortly before a competition. The athlete will have donated the blood a few weeks earlier, long enough so that like any other donor's, her blood supply will have returned to normal. The additional red cells packed in boost the ability of her blood to transport oxygen. More oxygen gets to the muscles readily. World-ranked runners can increase their speed up to about 2 per cent – but as records are judged in milliseconds this boost can be crucial. Athletes further down the scale may be boosted by up to 5 per cent.

Olympic runners of both sexes have been accused, and several of the cyclists on the American 1984 Olympic team, which won nine medals, are believed to have been helped by blood-doping.

Gymnasts in the East and the West stave off puberty to maintain their childlike flexibility and shape, but they maintain this is done without drugs (see Chapter 6, Killer Gymnastics).

Athletes started taking drugs before they were banned and before anyone knew what kinds of physical problems they caused. Male weightlifters and throwers were the first and worst offenders. At the 1972 Munich Olympics, two-thirds of the male discus throwers admitted having taken anabolic steroids. At the next Olympics in Montreal, seven male weightlifters and one female discus thrower, Danuta Rosani of Poland, failed the test for steroids. Because of the competition timetable, it was she who became the first athlete ever disqualified from competition at the Olympics. This pointed the finger at women as drug abusers, although seven times as many men had been shown to be guilty.

There is now random drug-testing at all major competitions and at many small ones. Those who are caught taking banned drugs are banned for a time from their sport – cynics say that time off gives them another chance to get on the drug for a good long bout undetected.

Athletes and coaches are getting expert advice from sport scientists and doctors who specialize in sport on what drugs to take, and when, in order to avoid detection. To avoid being caught, athletes now take banned drugs in cycles, leaving enough time off before competition, so that when they are tested they will be found to be 'clean'. Human Chorionic Gonadotrophin, derived from the urine of pregnant women, and designed to treat infertility, can be taken to stimulate the body's production of testosterone, which is banned only if taken as a foreign substance.

Another ploy increasingly used to outwit the drug tests is to take masking drugs which conceal traces of steroids in their urine. One such is Probenecid, designed for treating gout, which was banned late in 1987. Another is said to be cider vinegar.

Testing has become more sophisticated and thorough with time. But, if it is getting harder to cheat with drugs at sport because of the tests, it is also getting harder to detect cheating.

Sex testing for women

No man has ever been found impersonating a woman in the twenty years that women at the Olympics have been tested to make sure they are not men. Sex testing of women (but not men) is an embodiment of all the antiquated prejudices and suspicions against women in sport. It has always been controversial.

It was introduced when women's records began gaining noticeably on those of men. Muscular women had always taken part in the Olympics, but now there were more of them, and because of television coverage, more people were getting a look at them.

Sport was also a more serious business than ever, so athletes of both sexes trained hard and got bulkier. But only women were penalized for this development. The notion that men were better than women at sport was used to put women who were good at sport under suspicion.

The sex test was introduced in 1966 and was first used at the Olympics in 1968. Early on, women lined up naked and a team of doctors took a good look, inside and out. Then, a chromosome test was introduced.

In 1967, at the European Cup in Kiev, the Polish runner Eva Klobukowska became the first woman to pass that very thorough visual examination, but fail the genetic test. Most men have XY chromosomes, most women have XX. Klobukowska had an XXY. It was announced that she had 'one chromosome too many to be declared a woman for the purposes of athletic competition'. Eva Klobukowska, who looked to a team of medical specialists like a woman, and who had always lived as one, whose extra chromosome gave her no advantage at sport, was stripped of her records and banned from competing against women.

The sex test has remained controversial, and in 1986 a geneticist writing in the *Journal of the American Medical Association (JAMA)* criticized the fairness and the *validity* of the test. 'The present screening method is both inaccurate and discriminatory, in that it excludes women who should be allowed to participate,' wrote Dr Albert de la Chappelle of the Department of Medical Genetics at the University of Helsinki. He was referring to the six women in every thousand like Klobukowska, whose body composition, including muscle, is entirely female, except for that Y-chromosome.

Certain conditions that would give advantage do not show up in the chromosome tests. One such is adrenal hyperlasia, a hormonal imbalance, which gives one woman in five thousand, who has female genitalia, the shape and muscular strength of a man.

Dr de la Chappelle was not a lone voice in the wilderness. The leader, or editorial, of *JAMA* called for an end to sex tests on the grounds that 'eliminating screening would probably have little or no effect' on who won championships, 'and might restore a few personal dignities'.

Only a handful of masquerades have ever been uncovered in sport, most of them pre-dating the sex tests. In 1938 a German high-jumper was found to be an hermaphrodite, with both male and female sexual organs. Two Frenchwomen on the relay team which won silver at the 1946 European championship later were found to be living as men, but whether they had pretended to be women or were now pretending to be men was not completely certain. A skier who failed the chromosome test in the same year as Klobukowska had had her male sex organs hidden inside her body since birth. In 1980, the elderly Mrs Stella Olsen, a Polish-American, who had been the 1932 Olympic 100-metre sprint champion as Stanislawa Walasiewicz and had won forty-two American national titles as Stella Walsh, was killed, an innocent bystander in a robbery, and it was discovered that she had male sex organs.

Some athletes dropped out of competition when sex testing was about to start, but there is no proof that this is the reason they stopped competing. The most famous case was that of the most successful sisters in Olympic history, Irina and Tamara Press of the Soviet Union. Irina was the Olympic pentathlon and hurdles champion; Tamara the discus and shot-putting champion. When they quit, some people thought they must be men in disguise. But both had been at the top far longer than most champions. It is hard to keep training for years at peak intensity, and there is a tradition of retiring at the top. The Presses, who continue to live as women, may have decided to retire for these or for other legitimate reasons. On the other hand, they may have been men.

With this information at his disposal, Dr Daniel Hanley, the US representative to the IOC's medical committee, in 1985 called sex testing 'an expensive overreaction to a remote possibility.'

How can 'amateurs' make so much money?

Being an amateur, is, like everything else, a matter of definition.

According to the Victorian ideal, the Olympics were open to gentlemen who competed for the love of the game, not money. (They, of course, had private incomes and didn't need it.) Thereafter, not all Olympic athletes were gentlemen, but they were all supposed to be amateurs. Anyone who earned money from sport lost her or his amateur standing.

Over the last eighty years there has been a war of attrition against the amateur ideal, which has all but gone from sport. As the world standard went up, top competitors found they had to train full time. Many also had to earn a living, but all they had time for and all they were trained to do was sport. Yet getting paid for sport was against the rules of amateurism. Many athletes accepted payments secretly. It came in the form of appearance money, secret bonuses for winning world records, salaries for jobs at which athletes never turned up, and so forth. A large number of up-and-coming athletes still register as unemployed and receive government payments.

Because of under-cover payments in the West and widespread support of their athletes by governments in the Eastern bloc, the term amateur became inappropriate. There was talk of 'shamateurs' – athletes who accepted under-the-table payments.

The first widely criticised female Olympic 'shamateur', the great Babe Didrikson, was employed by an insurance company, supposedly as a typist. But her salary was for playing basketball for the winning company team and for training for the 1932 Olympics, where she was victorious in running, jumping and throwing events. The insurance company paid all her expenses at the Olympic trials and at the Games.

Tennis-players Suzanne Lenglen and Helen Wills Moody, swimmers Dawn Fraser and Sharron Davies and runner Mary Decker Slaney are but a few other athletes who were suspected of 'shamateurism' Amateurism hád become a sham.

In 1982 the IAAF ended this hypocrisy by agreeing that track and field athletes could be paid openly for sponsorship and advertising deals. The following year, the IAAF also agreed they could receive appearance money. The regulations tend to require that the money go into trust funds from which only 'expenses' are drawn until the athlete ends his or her career. Expenses may include a snazzy new car, down-payment on a house, or a winter training stint in the tropics.

This new state of affairs in which athletes can earn money is called open athletics. It has put an end to the hypocrisy of 'shamateurism'. Other sports have followed suit. And when tennis was welcomed back to the Olympics (see pp. 4 and 6), it was presumed that top pro players would compete, although they would not be able to compete for money within the two weeks immediately preceding the 1988 Games.

Winning a gold medal at the Olympics is still the peak of sporting achievement. But a large number of young athletes now want to become an Olympic champion because there is money in it.

Politics

Sport has never ever been separate from politics. Olympic boycotts and ugly incidents go way back. The Hitler Olympics of 1936 were a propaganda feast (see Chapter 3, Nazi Foil). The Netherlands was one of the countries to pull out of the 1956 Melbourne Games to protest against the Soviet invasion of Hungary and the British and French invasion of the Suez canal. In 1968 a threatened boycott by Black African nations forced the IOC to reverse its decision to readmit South Africa, and at the Games, two black male American athletes gave the Black Power salute. Palestinian terrorists murdered Israeli athletes at the 1972 Games in Munich – now there is careful security. In 1980 the United States showed its disapproval of the Soviet occupation of Afghanistan by boycotting the Moscow Olympics. Many Western allies followed suit. In 1984 most Eastern bloc countries boycotted the Los Angeles Olympics. Tit for tat.

These boycotts are hated by the athletes, who after all have given years of their life to prepare for the Games. Many feel they have been chosen as sacrifices because they are less powerful than corporate interests. In 1980, for example, the United States allowed American businessmen to continue their profitable trade with the Soviet Union.

At their most basic, too, the Games are political, since athletes compete on national teams, and victories at the Olympics are regarded as enhancing national prestige (see Chapter 1, Elbowing In, pp. 10 and 18). Nonetheless, there is a modicum of truth to the notion that the Games promote international understanding among youth. Athletes of all nations continue to enjoy competing together. They don't at all mind learning better techniques from each other, and they play by the same rules.

Television

Television, which has changed sport so much, is a surprisingly recent development. The 1960 Olympic Games in Rome were the first to be televised worldwide. In 1972 the TV cameras made Olga Korbut a star (see Chapter 6, Killer Gymnastics). At the 1988 Winter Olympics in Calgary, the timetable was stretched to three weekends as a condition of the $309 million ABC Television contract for North American rights. The fee was more than three times the rate for the 1984 Winter Games.

American TV then tried to reorder the timetables of major finals at Seoul to coincide with American prime viewing time. Since this would have put athletics finals on between nine and eleven in the morning, Korean time – not the best time for the athletes – the International Amateur Athletics Association said no. Then so did the IOC. The Americans' offer of $750 million was reduced but the final fee was well over twice the $270 million paid for Los Angeles.

Two and a half billion people, linked by satellite television, watched the 1984 Los Angeles Olympics; an even larger audience is expected for Seoul. In its bid to become the 1992 Olympic city, Amsterdam offered twenty-four hours of worldwide television each day.

Millions of people who have never been to a stadium now watch athletics, gymnastics, ice skating, skiing, equestrian and other sports at weekends, often on weekdays too. Television has brought many sports to a much bigger audience, no bad thing.

But it has also made us impatient with watching entire events – we are used to cutting to the highlights like the sports reports do. Television has also taught us to rely on one of its most clever inventions, the action replay. Seeing the important moments more than once was not possible before the camera arrived at the stadium.

Television has brought its own and the sponsors' money into sport. Many world-ranked athletes have become famous and rich, but some, like Mary Decker Slaney (see Chapter 9, Collision

Course), have seen their popularity founder because they failed to be champions when it came to handling the media.

Who are the greatest athletes in the world?

Heptathletes and their male counterparts, the decathletes, say it has to be them. Their sport is an all-round event, consisting of seven events over two days (decathletes do ten). Heptathletes have to master all of the athletics disciplines, running, jumping and throwing.

Versatility is only one of the keys to the heptathlon. Because there are so many different events involved, you need plenty of stamina and strength and perseverence.

On the first day a heptathlete has four events. First comes a 100-metres hurdle race. Next she puts the shot. Then comes the long-drawn-out high-jump competition. The last event of her day is another running event, the 200-metres race. It must be run flat out. If she has pushed herself hard, as is necessary for success, she will feel exhausted. But there is more to come on the second day.

Only three events today, but they include the lot – jumping, throwing and running. The day begins with the long jump. Then comes the javelin, and to finish with, an 800-metre race. You get points for each event. The highest total wins.

In Los Angeles in 1984, an Australian named Glynis Nunn became the first Olympic heptathlon champion. But the American heptathlete Jackie Joyner was soon ranked highest in the world, and in 1986 in Texas, she set her world record of a whopping 7,161 points (see page 36).

The heptathlon has superseded the pentathlon, which in the past was the women's mixed event; it consisted of only five disciplines. Because most people did not think it was a fair parallel with the decathlon, it was decided to give women a chance at the more demanding heptathlon. The last Olympic pentathlon was in Moscow in 1980.

The counter-argument points out that athletes who specialize in a single event are usually better at it than the multi-event athlete is. A world champion heptathlete, for example, will not be as good at shot-putting as the shot put world champion is. For this reason, the argument as to who really is the greatest will probably go on forever.

OLYMPIC RECORDS: SPORT BY SPORT IN PERSPECTIVE

Despite the erroneous 'better judgement' of a great many people, women made their Olympic debut at the 1900 Paris Games. The pleasant Miss Cooper of England decorously won the tennis, becoming the first woman champion of the modern Games. Her victory unleashed a firestorm of female energy.

The records here of gold medallists start at the first Olympic appearance of each event for women. During the war years of 1916, 1940 and 1944 there were no Games. Other missing years within lists indicate sports or events which were discontinued for a time and later reinstated. A space has been left in the record table for each event, to allow you to fill in the 1988 gold medal winners at Seoul.

Among new sports for women at Seoul in 1988: tennis (fully fledged), table tennis and judo (a demonstration event). There are also new events in sports in which women already compete, including, on the track, the 10,000 metres; in the pool, the 50-metres freestyle; at sea, the 470 yachting event; on the shooting range, the air pistol; on the bicycle, the 1,000-metres sprint; and team events in rowing and in archery.

New open events, in which women compete against men, are Olympic trap and skeet shooting and a division II yachting event replacing the wind-glider.

New events at the Winter Games in Calgary, where there were sixteen events for women, twenty-eight for men and two pairs competitions, included a combined downhill and slalom in skiing and a 5,000-metres speed-skating race. Calgary's highlights surely were Yvonne van Gennip's three speed skating golds and Katarina Witt's figure skating. Both East and West attended as they seem set to do at Seoul.

ARCHERY

The renowned five-times-Wimbledon-champion Charlotte 'Lottie' Dod (1871–1960), long since retired, picked up the 1908 silver medal in archery at the ripe old age of thirty-seven. In 1984 Seo Hyang-Soon of Korea became the sport's youngest gold medallist at seventeen years thirty-four days old. Men's archery entered the Games in 1900.

1904	*Double National Round*				
	Lida Howell (USA)	1908	*National Round*	1980	Keto Losaberidze (URS) 2491pts
	Double Columbia Round		Queenie Newall (GBR)	1984	Seo Hyang-Soon (KOR) 2568pts
	Lida Howell (USA)		*Double Fita Round*		*Team*
	Team Round	1972	Doreen Wilber (USA) 2424pts	1988	
	Cincinatti Archery Club (USA)	1976	Luann Ryon (USA) 2499pts		

ATHLETICS (TRACK & FIELD)

Track and field events, the keystone of the Olympics since 1896, were thought to be unnatural, unbecoming and dangerous for the 'weaker' sex. Women finally elbowed into the Games in 1928. Discus thrower Halina Konopacka of Poland was the first gold medallist.

The briefer the distance, the faster a runner can go because she doesn't have to sustain the pace for a long time. The winner of the 100 metres, less than eleven seconds on the track, is regarded as the fastest woman in the world. Her speed is roughly 25 miles per hour.

Long distances for women have been resisted by the International Olympic Committee ever since the notorious 800-metres race of 1928 (see Chapter 1, Elbowing In). The marathon is 26 miles 385 yards over streets and roads, ending in the Olympic stadium. Because of the varying road conditions in the marathon, only world best performances, not world records are recognized officially. It is not a distinction usually made in conversation. The first women's marathon was not till 1984; men ran the event at the very first modern Games.

100 Metres

1928	Elizabeth Robinson (USA) 12.2
1932	Stanislawa Walasiewicz (POL) 11.9
1936	Helen Stephens (USA) 11.5
1948	Fanny Blankers-Koen (HOL) 11.9
1952	Marjorie Jackson (AUS) 11.5
1956	Betty Cuthbert (AUS) 11.5
1960	Wilma Rudolph (USA) 11.0
1964	Wyomia Tyus (USA) 11.4
1968	Wyomia Tyus (USA) 11.0
1972	Renate Stecher (GDR) 11.07
1976	Annegret Richter (FRG) 11.08
1980	Ludmila Kondratyeva (URS) 11.06
1984	Evelyn Ashford (USA) 10.97
1988	

200 Metres

1948	Fanny Blankers-Koen (HOL) 24.4
1952	Marjorie Jackson (AUS) 23.7
1956	Betty Cuthbert (AUS) 23.4
1960	Wilma Rudolph (USA) 24.0
1964	Edith Maguire (USA) 23.0
1968	Irena Szewinska (POL) 22.5
1972	Renate Stecher (GDR) 22.40
1976	Barbel Eckert (GDR) 22.37
1980	Barbel Wöckel (GDR) 22.03
1984	Valerie Brisco-Hooks (USA) 21.81
1988	

400 Metres

1964	Betty Cuthbert (AUS) 52.0
1968	Colette Besson (FRA) 52.0
1972	Monika Zehrt (GDR) 51.08
1976	Irena Szewinska (POL) 49.29
1980	Marita Koch (GDR) 48.88
1984	Valerie Brisco-Hooks (USA) 48.83
1988	

800 Metres

1928	Lina Radke (GER) 2:16.8
1960	Ludmila Shevtsova (URS) 2:04.3
1964	Ann Packer (GBR) 2:01.1
1968	Madeline Manning (USA) 2:00.9
1972	Hildegard Falck (FRG) 1:58.6
1976	Tatyana Kazankina (URS) 1:54.9
1980	Nadyezda Olizarenko (URS) 1:53.5
1984	Doina Melinte (ROM) 1:57.60
1988	

1500 Metres

1972	Ludmila Brágina (URS) 4:01.4
1976	Tatyana Kazankina (URS) 4:05.5
1980	Tatyana Kazankina (URS) 3:56.6
1984	Gabriella Dorio (ITA) 4:03.25
1988	

3000 Metres

1984	Maricica Puica (ROM) 8:35.96
1988	

10 000 Metres

1988	

Marathon

1984	Joan Benoit (USA) 2h 24:52
1988	

100 Metres Hurdles

(Over 80m hurdles 1932–1968)

1932	Mildred Didrikson (USA) 11.7
1936	Trebisonda Valla (ITA) 11.7
1948	Fanny Blankers-Koen (HOL) 11.2
1952	Shirley de la Hunty (AUS) 10.9
1956	Shirley de la Hunty (AUS) 10.7
1960	Irina Press (URS) 10.8 (10.93)
1964	Karin Balzer (GER) 10.5 (10.54)
1968	Maureen Caird (AUS) 10.3
1972	Annelie Ehrhardt (GDR) 12.59
1976	Johanna Schaller (GDR) 12.77
1980	Vera Komisova (URS) 12.56
1984	Benita Fitzgerald-Brown (USA) 12.84
1988	

400 Metres Hurdles

1984	Nawal El Moutawakel (MAR) 54.61
1988	

4 × 100 Metres Relay

1928	Canada 48.4
1932	United States 47.0
1936	United States 46.9
1948	Netherlands 47.5
1952	United States 45.9
1956	Australia 44.5
1960	United States 44.5
1964	Poland 43.6 (43.69)
1968	United States 42.8
1972	FRG 42.81
1976	GDR 42.55

1980	GDR 41.60	
1984	United States 41.65	
1988		

4 × 400 Metres Relay

1972	GDR 3:22.95
1976	GDR 3:19.23
1980	Soviet Union 3:20.12
1984	United States 3:18.29
1988	

High Jump

1928	Ethel Catherwood (CAN) 1.59m
1932	Jean Shiley (USA) 1.65m
1936	Ibolya Csák (HUN) 1.60m
1948	Alice Coachman (USA) 1.68m
1952	Esther Brand (SAF) 1.67m
1956	Mildred McDaniel (USA) 1.76m
1960	Iolanda Balas (ROM) 1.85m
1964	Iolanda Balas (ROM) 1.90m
1968	Miloslava Rezkova (TCH) 1.82m
1972	Ulrike Meyfarth (FRG) 1.92m
1976	Rosemarie Ackermann (GDR) 1.93m
1980	Sara Simeoni (ITA) 1.97m
1984	Ulrike Meyfarth (FRG) 2.02m
1988	

Long Jump

1948	Olga Gyarmati (HUN) 5.69m
1952	Yvette Williams (NZL) 6.24m
1956	Elzbieta Krzesinska (POL) 6.35m
1960	Vera Krepkina (URS) 6.37m

1964	Mary Rand (GBR) 6.76m
1968	Viorica Viscopoleanu (ROM) 6.82m
1972	Heidemarie Rosendahl (FRG) 6.78m
1976	Angela Voigt (GDR) 6.72m
1980	Tatyana Kolpakova (URS) 7.06m
1984	Anisoara Stanciu (ROM) 6.96m
1988	

Shot Put

1948	Micheline Ostermeyer (FRA) 13.75m
1952	Galina Zybina (URS) 15.28m
1956	Tamara Tyshkevich (URS) 16.59m
1960	Tamara Press (URS) 17.32m
1964	Tamara Press (URS) 18.14m
1968	Margitta Gummel (GDR) 19.61m
1972	Nadyezda Chizhova (URS) 21.03m
1976	Ivanka Khristova (BUL) 21.16m
1980	Ilona Slupianek (GDR) 22.41m
1984	Claudia Losch (FRG) 20.48m
1988	

Discus

1928	Halina Konopacka (POL) 39.62m
1932	Lillian Copeland (USA) 40.58m
1936	Gisela Mauermayer (GER) 47.63m
1948	Micheline Ostermeyer (FRA) 41.92m
1952	Nina Romashkova (URS) 51.42m
1956	Olga Fikotova (TCH) 53.69m
1960	Nina Ponomaryeva (URS) 55.10m
1964	Tamara Press (URS) 57.27m
1968	Lia Manoliu (ROM) 58.28m
1972	Faina Melnik (URS) 66.62

1976	Evelin Schlaak (GDR) 69.00m
1980	Evelin Jahl (GDR) 69.96m
1984	Ria Stalman (HOL) 65.36m
1988	

Javelin

1932	Mildred Didrikson (USA) 43.68m
1936	Tilly Fleischer (GER) 45.18m
1948	Herma Bauma (AUT) 45.57m
1952	Dana Zatopkova (TCH) 50.47m
1956	Ines Jaunzeme (URS) 53.86m
1960	Elvira Ozolina (URS) 55.98m
1964	Mihaela Penes (ROM) 60.64m
1968	Angela Németh (HUN) 60.36m
1972	Ruth Fuchs (GDR) 63.88m
1976	Ruth Fuchs (GDR) 65.94m
1980	Maria Colon (CUB) 68.40m
1984	Tessa Sanderson (GBR) 69.56m
1988	

Pentathlon

1964	Irina Press (URS) 5246pts
1968	Ingrid Becker (FRG) 5098pts
1972	Mary Peters (GBR) 4801pts
1976	Siegrun Siegl (GDR) 4745pts
1980	Nadyezda Tkachenko (URS) 5083pts

Heptathlon

(Replaced Pentathlon in 1984)

1984	Glynis Nunn (AUS) 6390pts
1988	

BASKETBALL

The tallest and heaviest female Olympic champion in any sport was Iuliana Semenova, the Soviet team captain, at 7 feet 1¾ inches tall and 284 lbs. Men's basketball entered the Games in 1936.

1976	Soviet Union	1984	United States
1980	Soviet Union	1988	

CANOEING

The great kayakers so far have been from Scandinavia or Eastern Europe. The woman who has won the most gold medals is Ludmila Khvedosyuk Pinayeva, who won three – one under her maiden, two under her married name. Men's canoeing entered the Games in 1936 and has many more events.

500 Metres Kayak Singles (K1)

1948	Karen Hoff (DEN) 2:31.9
1952	Sylvi Saimo (FIN) 2:18.4
1956	Elisaveta Dementyeva (URS) 2:18.9
1960	Antonina Seredina (URS) 2:08.08
1964	Ludmila Khvedosyuk (URS) 2:12.87
1968	Ludmila Pinayeva (URS) 2:11.09
1972	Yulia Ryabchinskaya (URS) 2:03.17
1976	Carola Zirzow (GDR) 2:01.05
1980	Birgit Fischer (GDR) 1:57.96
1984	Agneta Andersson (SWE) 1:58.72
1988	

500 Metres Kayak Pairs (K2)

1960	Soviet Union 1:54.76
1964	Germany 1:56.95
1968	FRG 1:56.44
1972	Soviet Union 1:53.50
1976	Soviet Union 1:51.15
1980	GDR 1:43.88
1984	Sweden 1:45.25
1988	

500 Metres Kayak Fours (K4)

1984	Romania 1:38.34
1988	

Slalom Racing Kayak Singles (K1)

(Discontinued for both sexes)

1972	Angelika Bahmann (GDR) 364.50

CYCLING

In 1984, the first cycling event for women was introduced. At that Olympics, there were seven events for men. Men's cycling entered the Games in 1896.

Individual road race (79.2 km)

1984	Connie Carpenter-Phinney (USA) 2:11.14
1988	

1000 Metres

1988	

EQUESTRIAN SPORT

Even in medieval tapestries women rode alongside men. But the Olympics admitted them only reluctantly. All-male showjumping entered the Games in 1900; all-male dressage and three-day eventing in 1912. In 1952 the first four women competed (against men) in dressage – one of them, Lis Hartel of Denmark, won silver. She did it again in 1962. In 1956 a female showjumper shared the team bronze medal and women have now won individual silver and bronze medals. In three-day eventing, the first woman (and there was only one) competed in 1964; in 1972 there were two women on the gold medal winning team; by 1984 one-third of the eventers were female – and they won two of the three individual medals.

Grand Prix (Dressage)

1952	Henri St Cyr (SWE) 561pts *Master Rufus*
1956	Henri St Cyr (SWE) 860pts *Juli*
1960	Sergey Filatov (URS) 2144pts *Absent*
1964	Henri Chammartin (SUI) 1504pts *Woermann*
1968	Ivan Kizimov (URS) 1572pts *Ikhov*
1972	Liselott Linsenhoff (FRG) 1229pts *Piaff*
1976	Christine Stückelberger (SUI) 1486pts *Granat*
1980	Elisabeth Theurer (AUT) 1370pts *Mon Cherie*
1984	Reiner Klimke (FRG) 1504pts *Ahlerich*
1988	

Grand Prix (Dressage) Team

1952	Sweden 1597.5pts
1956	Sweden 2475pts
1964	Germany 2558pts
1968	FRG 2699pts
1972	Soviet Union 5095pts
1976	FRG 5155pts
1980	Soviet Union 4383pts
1984	FRG 4955pts
1988	

Grand Prix (Jumping)

1968	William Steinkraus (USA) 4 faults *Snowbound*
1972	Graziano Mancinelli (ITA) 8 faults *Ambassador*
1976	Alwin Schockemöhle (FRG) no faults *Warwick Rex*
1980	Jan Kowalczyk (POL) 8 faults *Artemor*
1984	Joe Fargis (USA) 4 faults *Touch of Class*
1988	

Grand Prix (Jumping) Team

1956	Germany 40 faults
1960	Germany 46.50 faults
1964	Germany 68.50 faults
1968	Canada 102.75 faults
1972	FRG 32 faults
1976	France 40 faults
1980	Soviet Union 16 faults
1984	United States 12 faults
1988	

Three-day Event

1964	Mauro Checcoli (ITA) 64.40pts *Surbean*
1968	Jean-Jacques Guyon (FRA) 38.86pts *Pitou*
1972	Richard Meade (GBR) 57.73pts *Laurieston*
1976	Edmund Coffin (USA) 114.99pts *Bally-Cor*
1980	Federico Roman (ITA) 108.60pts *Rossinan*
1984	Mark Todd (NZL) 51.60pts *Charisma*
1988	

Three-day Event Team

1964	Italy 85.80pts
1968	Great Britain 175.93pts
1972	Great Britain 95.53pts
1976	United States 441.00pts
1980	Soviet Union 457.00pts
1984	United States 186.00pts
1988	

FENCING

Once the gentlemanly means of settling disputes, fencing competition for men – in foil and sabre – took place at the first modern Olympics in 1896. Men's epée was added the next time round. Women were to wait until 1924 for individual foil and 1960 for team foil competition.

Foil (Individual)

1924	Ellen Osiier (DEN) 5 wins
1928	Hélène Mayer (GER) 7 wins
1932	Ellen Preis (AUT) 9 wins
1936	Ilona Elek (HUN) 6 wins
1948	Ilona Elek (HUN) 6 wins
1952	Irene Camber (ITA) 5 wins
1956	Gillian Sheen (GBR) 6 wins
1960	Heidi Schmid (GER) 6 wins
1964	Ildikó Ujlaki-Rejtö (HUN) 2 wins
1968	Elena Novikova (URS) 4 wins
1972	Antonella Ragno-Lonzi (ITA) 4 wins
1976	Ildikó Schwarczenberger (HUN) 4 wins
1980	Pascale Trinquet (FRA) 4 wins
1984	Jujie Luan (CHN)
1988	

Foil (Team)

1960	Soviet Union
1964	Hungary
1968	Soviet Union
1972	Soviet Union
1976	Soviet Union
1980	France
1984	FRG
1988	

GOLF (discontinued for both sexes)

A game with an even longer history than tennis. One wonders when it too will return to the Olympics.

1904	Margaret Abbott (USA)

GYMNASTICS

Despite the present feminine aura of this sport, women's gymnastics did not enter the Olympics until 1928 and then only with team competition. The first individual medals were in 1952. Men's gymnastics had been there from the start.

Grace and fluidity are what a gymnast is credited with; but it is muscle which gives her control. Her legs will be visibly muscular. Courage is increasingly necessary, as since the advent of Olga Korbut and Nadia Comaneci, who introduced many 'risk values', the sport has deserved its tag of Killer Gymnastics.

Individual Combined Exercises (Overall Champion)

1952	Maria Gorokhovskaya (URS) 76.78
1956	Larissa Latynina (URS) 74.933
1960	Larissa Latynina (URS) 77.031
1964	Vera Caslavska (TCH) 77.564
1968	Vera Caslavska (TCH) 78.25
1972	Ludmila Tourischeva (URS) 77.025
1976	Nadia Comaneci (ROM) 79.275
1980	Elena Davydova (URS) 79.150
1984	Mary Lou Retton (USA) 79.175
1988	

1972	Olga Korbut (URS) 19.575
1976	Nadia Comaneci (ROM) 19.950
1980	Nadia Comaneci (ROM) 19.800
1984	Simona Pauca (ROM) and
	Ecaterina Szabo (ROM) 19.800
1988	

1964	Vera Caslavska (TCH) 19.483
1968	Vera Caslavska (TCH) 19.775
1972	Karin Janz (GDR) 19.525
1976	Nelli Kim (URS) 19.800
1980	Natalya Shaposhnikova (URS) 19.725
1984	Ecaterina Szabo (ROM) 19.875
1988	

Asymmetrical Bars

1952	Margit Korondi (HUN) 19.40
1956	Agnes Keleti (HUN) 18.966
1960	Polina Astakhova (URS) 19.616
1964	Polina Astakhova (URS) 19.332
1968	Vera Caslavska (TCH) 19.650
1972	Karin Janz (GDR) 19.675
1976	Nadia Comaneci (ROM) 20.000
1980	Maxi Gnauck (GDR) 19.875
1984	Ma Yanhong (CHN) and
	Julianne McNamara (USA) 19.950
1988	

Floor Exercises

1952	Agnes Keleti (HUN) 19.36
1956	Larissa Latynina (URS) 18.733
	Agnes Keleti (HUN) 18.733
1960	Larissa Latynina (URS) 19.583
1964	Larissa Latynina (URS) 19.599
1968	Larissa Petrik (URS) 19.675
	Vera Caslavska (TCH) 19.675
1972	Olga Korbut (URS) 19.575
1976	Nelli Kim (URS) 19.850
1980	Nelli Kim (URS) 19.875
	Nadia Comaneci (ROM) 19.875
1984	Ecaterina Szabo (ROM) 19.975
1988	

Team

1928	Netherlands 316.75pts
1936	Germany 506.50pts
1948	Czechoslovakia 445.45pts
1952	Soviet Union 527.03pts
1956	Soviet Union 444.80pts
1960	Soviet Union 382.320pts
1964	Soviet Union 380.890pts
1968	Soviet Union 382.85pts
1972	Soviet Union 380.50pts
1976	Soviet Union 390.35pts
1980	Soviet Union 394.90pts
1984	Romania 392.20pts
1988	

Balance Beam

1952	Nina Bocharova (URS) 19.22
1956	Agnes Keleti (HUN) 18.80
1960	Eva Bosakova (TCH) 19.283
1964	Vera Caslavska (TCH) 19.449
1968	Natalya Kuchinskaya (URS) 19.650

Horse Vault

1952	Yekaterina Kalinchuk (URS) 19.20
1956	Larissa Latynina (URS) 18.833
1960	Margarita Nikolayeva (URS) 19.316

Modern Rhythmic

1984	Lori Fung (CAN) 57.950
1988	

HOCKEY

In the 1880s, women played hockey at Oxford and Cambridge. In 1901, women students played at Harvard Summer School – and soon after at Vassar. Yet it took until 1980 for women's hockey to be admitted to the Games. Men's hockey was introduced in 1908.

1980	Zimbabwe	1984	Netherlands	1988	

JUDO

Men's judo entered the Games in 1964. Competitors and organizers of the men's Judo Federation agreed to relinquish one weight category to gain admission for women's judo as a demonstration sport in 1988.

1988	

169

LUGE (TOBOGANNING)

Aside from the odd one-man skeleton sledge race, both men's and women's lugeing entered the Games in 1964.

1964	Ortrun Enderlein (GER) 3:24.67	1976	Margit Schumann (GDR) 2:50.621	Steffi Walter (GDR) 3:03.973	
1968	Erica Lechner (ITA) 2:28.66	1980	Vera Sosulya (URS) 2:36.537		
1972	Anna-Maria Müller (GDR) 2:59.18	1984	Steffi Martin (GDR) 2:46.570		

ROWING

In 1900 at the Paris Olympics, men rowed on the Seine. American college women had already been rowing for a quarter of a century. It was only in 1976 that women's Olympic rowing was introduced with six events (the men had eight) over a 1,000-metre course, going up to 2,000 metres in 1988.

Rowing
Single Sculls

1976	Christine Scheiblich (GDR) 4:05.56
1980	Sandra Toma (ROM) 3:40.69
1984	Valeria Racila (ROM) 3:40.68
1988	

Coxless Pairs

1976	Bulgaria 4:01.22
1980	GDR 3:30.49
1984	Romania 3:32.60
1988	

Coxed Fours

1976	GDR 3:45.08
1980	GDR 3:19.27
1984	Romania 3:19.30
1988	

Double Sculls

1976	Bulgaria 3:44.36
1980	Soviet Union 3:16.27
1984	Romania 3:26.75
1988	

Coxed Quadruple Sculls

1976	GDR 3:29.99
1980	GDR 3:15.32
1984	Romania 3:14.11

Eights

1976	GDR 3:33.32
1980	GDR 3:03.32
1984	United States 2:59.80
1988	

Coxless Quadruple Sculls

1988	

SHOOTING

Shooting was one of the original Olympic events. Daringly, Mexico, Peru and Poland had women in their teams at the 1964 Olympics. The first of the women to compete was Mexico's Nuria Ortiz, who finished thirteenth in skeet shooting. Outshooting a field of men in the 1976 small-bore rifle event, Margaret Murdock, an American, won a silver medal. The youngest medalist ever of either sex, Ulrike Holmer, a West German, was sixteen years 305 days old when she won silver in the 1984 women's standard rifle. Three events for women were introduced in 1984.

Sport Pistol

1984	Linda Thorn (CAN) 585
1988	

Standard Rifle

1984	Xiaoxuan Wu (CHN) 581
1988	

Air Rifle

1984	Pat Spurgin (USA) 393
1988	

Air Pistol

1988	

Olympic Trap & Skeet Shooting (Open Event)

1988	

SKATING (FIGURE)

In 1902 an uppity British woman named Madge Syers entered the world championships, supposedly only for men, and placed second. It was she who became the first female Olympic champion when the sport entered the Games six years later. Sonja Henie, who later made millions in ice shows and the movies, introduced jumps into the women's event. But when Theresa Weld, the 1920 bronze medallist, jumped a salchow she was warned against such 'unfeminine behaviour'. The ice dancers Jayne Torvill and Christopher Dean won in 1984 with a maximum nine sixes plus three sixes for technical merit – the highest score ever.

1908	Madge Syers (GBR) 1262.5pts
1920	Magda Julin-Mauroy (SWE) 913.5pts
1924	Herma Planck-Szabo (AUT) 2094.25pts
1928	Sonja Henie (NOR) 2452.25pts
1932	Sonja Henie (NOR) 2302.5pts
1936	Sonja Henie (NOR) 2971.4pts
1948	Barbara Scott (CAN) 1467.7pts

1952	Jeanette Altwegg (GBR) 1455.8pts			
1956	Tenley Albright (USA) 1866.39pts			
1960	Carol Heiss (USA) 1490.1pts			
1964	Sjoukje Dijkstra (HOL) 2018.5pts			
1968	Peggy Fleming (USA) 1970.5pts			
1972	Beatrix Schuba (AUT) 2751.5pts			
1976	Dorothy Hamill (USA) 193.80pts			
1980	Anett Pötzsch (GDR) 189.00pts			
1984	Katarina Witt (GDR) 3.2			
1988	Katarina Witt (GDR) 4.2			

Pairs

1908	Germany 56.0pts
1920	Finland 80.75pts
1924	Austria 74.50pts
1928	France 100.50pts
1932	France 76.7pts
1936	Germany 103.3pts
1948	Belgium 123.5pts
1952	Germany 102.6pts
1956	Austria 101.8pts
1960	Canada 80.4pts
1964	Soviet Union 104.4pts

1968	Soviet Union 315.2pts
1972	Soviet Union 420.4pts
1976	Soviet Union 140.54pts
1980	Soviet Union 147.26pts
1984	Soviet Union 1.4
1988	Soviet Union 1.4

Ice Dance

1976	Soviet Union 209.92pts
1980	Soviet Union 205.48pts
1984	Great Britain 2.0
1988	Soviet Union 2.0

SKATING (SPEED)

Introduced in 1924, though women were to wait until 1960. That year Lydia Skoblikova of the Soviet Union won two gold medals, then four more in 1964, a total of six, still the record for either sex and any sport in the Winter Games. Yvonne van Gennip's triple in Calgary was an equal accomplishment as the sport is now more competitive.

500 Metres

1960	Helga Haase (GER) 45.9
1964	Lydia Skoblikova (URS) 45.0
1968	Ludmila Titova (URS) 46.1
1972	Anne Henning (USA) 43.33
1976	Sheila Young (USA) 42.76
1980	Karin Enke (GDR) 41.78
1984	Christa Rothenburger (GDR) 41.02
1988	Bonnie Blair (USA) 39.10

1000 Metres

1960	Klara Guseva (URS) 1:34.1
1964	Lydia Skoblikova (URS) 1:33.2
1968	Carolina Geijssen (HOL) 1:32.6
1972	Monika Pflug (FRG) 1:31.40

1976	Tatyana Averina (URS) 1:28.43
1980	Natalya Petruseva (URS) 1:24.10
1984	Karin Enke (GDR) 1:21.61
1988	Christa Rothenburger (GDR) 1:17.65

1500 Metres

1960	Lydia Skoblikova (URS) 2:25.2
1964	Lydia Skoblikova (URS) 2:22.6
1968	Kaija Mustonen (FIN) 2:22.4
1972	Dianne Holum (USA) 2:20.85
1976	Galina Stepanskaya (URS) 2:16.58
1980	Annie Borckink (HOL) 2:10.95
1984	Karin Enke (GDR) 2:03.42
1988	Yvonne van Gennip (HOL) 2:00.68

3000 Metres

1960	Lydia Skoblikova (URS) 5:14.3
1964	Lydia Skoblikova (URS) 5:14.9
1968	Johanna Schut (HOL) 4:56.2
1972	Christina Baas-Kaiser (HOL) 4:52.14
1976	Tatyana Averina (URS) 4:45.19
1980	Björg Eva Jensen (NOR) 4:32.13
1984	Andrea Schoene (GDR) 4:24.79
1988	Yvonne van Gennip (HOL) 4:11.94

5000 Metres

1988	Yvonne van Gennip (HOL) 7:14.13

SKIING (ALPINE)

Four women have won double gold, the most recent being the world giant slalom champion Vreni Schneider, at Calgary. Two women have won gold medals at two games. Skiing entered the Games for both sexes in 1936.

Alpine Combination
(Downhill and Slalom)

1936	Christel Cranz (GER) 97.06pts
1948	Trude Beiser (AUT) 6.58pts
1988	Anita Wachter (AUT) 29.25pts

Slalom

1948	Gretchen Fraser (USA) 1:57.2
1952	Andrea Mead-Lawrence (USA) 2:10.6
1956	Renée Colliard (SUI) 1:52.3
1960	Anne Heggtveit (CAN) 1:49.6
1964	Christine Goitschel (FRA) 1:29.86
1968	Marielle Goitschel (FRA) 1:25.86
1972	Barbara Cochran (USA) 1:31.24
1976	Rosi Mittermaier (FRG) 1:30.54
1980	Hanni Wenzel (LIE) 1:25.09
1984	Paoletta Magoni (ITA) 1:36.47
1988	Vreni Schneider (SUI) 1:36.69

Giant Slalom

1952	Andrea Mead-Lawrence (USA) 2:06.8
1956	Ossi Reichert (GER) 1:56.5
1960	Yvonne Ruegg (SUI) 1:39.9
1964	Marielle Goitschel (FRA) 1:52.24
1968	Nancy Greene (CAN) 1:51.97
1972	Marie-Thérèse Nadig (SUI) 1:29.90
1976	Kathy Kreiner (CAN) 1:29.13
1980	Hanni Wenzel (LIE) 2:41.66
1984	Debbie Armstrong (USA) 2:20.98
1988	Vreni Schneider (SUI) 2:06.49

Super Giant Slalom

1988	Sigrid Wolf (AUT) 1:19.03

Downhill

1948	Hedy Schlunegger (SUI) 2:28.3
1952	Trude Jochum-Beiser (AUT) 1:47.1
1956	Madeleine Berthod (SUI) 1:40.7
1960	Heidi Biebl (GER) 1:37.6
1964	Christl Haas (AUT) 1:55.39
1968	Olga Pall (AUT) 1:40.87
1972	Marie-Thérèse Nadig (SUI) 1:36.68
1976	Rosi Mittermaier (FRG) 1:46.16
1980	Annemarie Moser-Pröll (AUT) 1:37.52
1984	Michela Figini (SUI) 1:13.36
1988	Marina Kiehl (FRG) 1:25.86

SKIING (CROSS-COUNTRY)

Cross-country (or Nordic) skiing has been an Olympic event for men since the first Winter Games in Chamonix in 1928. One women's event was introduced twenty-four years later.

5000 Metres

1964	Klaudia Boyarskikh (URS) 17:50.5
1968	Toini Gustafsson (SWE) 16:45.2
1972	Galina Kulakova (URS) 17:00.50
1976	Helena Takalo (FIN) 15:48.69
1980	Raisa Smetanina (URS) 15:06.92
1984	Marja-Liisa Hämäläinen (FIN) 17:04.0
1988	Marjo Matikainen (FIN) 15:4.0

10 000 Metres

1952	Lydia Wideman (FIN) 41:40.0
1956	Lubov Kozyryeva (URS) 38:11.0

1960	Maria Gusakova (URS) 39:46.6
1964	Klaudia Boyarskikh (URS) 40:24.3
1968	Toini Gustafsson (SWE) 36:46.5
1972	Galina Kulakova (URS) 34:17.8
1976	Raisa Smetanina (URS) 30:13.41
1980	Barbara Petzold (GDR) 30:31.54
1984	Marja-Liisa Hämäläinen (FIN) 31:44.2
1988	Vida Ventsene (URS) 30:08.3

20 000 Metres

1984	Marja-Liisa Hämäläinen (FIN) 1h 01:45.0
1988	Tamara Tikhonova (URS) 55:53.6

4 × 5000 Metres Relay

1956	Finland 1h 09:01.0
1960	Sweden 1h 04:21.4
1964	Soviet Union 59:20.2
1968	Norway 57:30.0
1972	Soviet Union 48:46.15
1976	Soviet Union 1h 07:49.75
1980	GDR 1h 02:11.10
1984	Norway 1h 06:49.7
1988	Soviet Union 59:51.1

SWIMMING & DIVING

One of the original Olympic sports, less reluctant than many to welcome women – a few competed in 1912. By 1984 each sex had 18 events (counting synchronized swimming and water polo). The record for the most individual gold medals won by a woman, the Australian Dawn Fraser's four in 1956–1972, was equalled by Kornelia Ender of East Germany in 1976. Fraser is the only swimmer of either sex to win the same event (100-metres freestyle) three times. In 1984, in that event, two women tied for gold; it was the first dead heat ever in an Olympic swimming final.

An Olympic pool has eight lanes and is 50 metres (about 164 feet) long. There are four racing strokes: freestyle (front crawl), butterfly, breaststroke, and backstroke. In a medley event, a swimmer does one or more laps of each stroke.

50 Metres Freestyle

1988

100 Metres Freestyle

1912	Fanny Durack (AUS) 1:22.2
1920	Ethelda Bleibtrey (USA) 1:13.6
1924	Ethel Lackie (USA) 1:12.4
1928	Albina Osipowich (USA) 1:11.0
1932	Helene Madison (USA) 1:06.8
1936	Henrika Mastenbroek (HOL) 1:05.9
1948	Greta Andersen (DEN) 1:06.3
1952	Katalin Szöke (HUN) 1:06.8
1956	Dawn Fraser (AUS) 1:02.0
1960	Dawn Fraser (AUS) 1:01.2
1964	Dawn Fraser (AUS) 59.5
1968	Jan Henne (USA) 1:00.0
1972	Sandra Neilson (USA) 58.59
1976	Kornelia Ender (GDR) 55.65
1980	Barbara Krause (GDR) 54.79
1984	Carrie Steinseifer (USA) 55.92
	Nancy Hogshead (USA) 55.92
1988	

200 Metres Freestyle

1968	Debbie Meyer (USA) 2:10.5
1972	Shane Gould (AUS) 2:03.56
1976	Kornelia Ender (GDR) 1:59.26
1980	Barbara Krause (GDR) 1:58.33
1984	Mary Wayte (USA) 1:59.23
1988	

400 Metres Freestyle

1920[1]	Ethelda Bleibtrey (USA) 4:34.0
1924	Martha Norelius (USA) 6:02.2
1928	Martha Norelius USA) 5:42.8
1932	Helene Madison (USA) 5:28.5

1936	Henrika Mastenbroek (HOL) 5:26.4
1948	Ann Curtis (USA) 5:17.8
1952	Valéria Gyenge (HUN) 5:12.1
1956	Lorraine Crapp (AUS) 4:54.6
1960	Chris von Saltza (USA) 4:50.6
1964	Virginia Duenkel (USA) 4:43.3
1968	Debbie Meyer (USA) 4:31.8
1972	Shane Gould (AUS) 4:19.04
1976	Petra Thuemer (GDR) 4:09.89
1980	Ines Diers (GDR) 4:08.76
1984	Tiffany Cohen (USA) 4:07.10
1988	

[1] 300 metres.

800 Metres Freestyle

1968	Debbie Meyer (USA) 9:24.0
1972	Keena Rothhammer (USA) 8:53.68
1976	Petra Thuemer (GDR) 8:37.14
1980	Michelle Ford (AUS) 8:28.90
1984	Tiffany Cohen (USA) 8:24.95
1988	

100 Metres Backstroke

1924	Sybil Bauer (USA) 1:23.2

1928	Marie Braun (HOL) 1:22.0
1932	Eleanor Holm (USA) 1:19.4
1936	Dina Senff (HOL) 1:18.9
1948	Karen Harup (DEN) 1:14.4
1952	Joan Harrison (SAF) 1:14.3
1956	Judy Grinham (GBR) 1:12.9
1960	Lynn Burke (USA) 1:09.3
1964	Cathy Ferguson (USA) 1:07.7
1968	Kaye Hall (USA) 1:06.2
1972	Melissa Belote (USA) 1:05.78
1976	Ulrike Richter (GDR) 1:01.83
1980	Rica Reinisch (GDR) 1:00.86
1984	Theresa Andrews (USA) 1:02.55
1988	

200 Metres Backstroke

1968	Lillian Watson (USA) 2:24.8
1972	Melissa Belote (USA) 2:19.19
1976	Ulrike Richter (GDR) 2:13.43
1980	Rica Reinisch (GDR) 2:11.77
1984	Jolanda De Rover (HOL) 2:12.38
1988	

100 Metres Breaststroke

1968	Djurdjica Bjedov (YUG) 1:15.8
1972	Catherine Carr (USA) 1:13.58
1976	Hannelore Anke (GDR) 1:11.16
1980	Ute Geweniger (GDR) 1:10.22
1984	Petra Van Staveren (HOL) 1:09.88
1988	

200 Metres Breaststroke

1924	Lucy Morton (GBR) 3:33.2
1928	Hilde Schrader (GER) 3:12.6
1932	Claire Dennis (AUS) 3:06.3
1936	Hideko Maehata (JPN) 3:03.6
1948	Petronella van Vliet (HOL) 2:57.2
1952	Eva Székely[1] (HUN) 2:51.7
1956	Ursula Happe[2] (GER) 2:53.1
1960	Anita Lonsbrough (GBR) 2:49.5
1964	Galina Prozumenshchikova (URS) 2:46.4
1968	Sharon Wichman (USA) 2:44.4
1972	Beverley Whitfield (AUS) 2:41.71
1976	Marina Kosheveya (URS) 2:33.35
1980	Lina Kachushite (URS) 2:29.54
1984	Anne Ottenbrite (CAN) 2:30.38
1988	

[1] Used then permitted [1]butterfly stroke,
[2] underwater technique.

100 Metres Butterfly

1956	Shelley Mann (USA) 1:11.0
1960	Carolyn Schuler (USA) 1:09.5
1964	Sharon Stouder (USA) 1:04.7
1968	Lynette McClements (AUS) 1:05.5
1972	Mayumi Aoki (JPN) 1:03.34
1976	Kornelia Ender (GDR) 1:00.13
1980	Caren Metschuck (GDR) 1:00.42
1984	Mary Meagher (USA) 59.26
1988	

* Olympic record 59.05 in heats.

200 Metres Butterfly

1968	Ada Kok (HOL) 2:24.7
1972	Karen Moe (USA) 2:15.57
1976	Andrea Pollack (GDR) 2:11.41
1980	Ines Geissler (GDR) 2:10.44
1984	Mary Meagher (USA) 2:06.90
1988	

200 Metres Individual Medley

1968	Claudia Kolb (USA) 2:24.7
1972	Shane Gould (AUS) 2:23.07
1984	Tracy Caulkins (USA) 2:12.64
1988	

400 Metres Individual Medley

1964	Donna De Varona (USA) 5:18.7
1968	Claudia Kolb (USA) 5:08.5
1972	Gail Neall (AUS) 5:02.97
1976	Ulrike Tauber (GDR) 4:42.77
1980	Petra Schneider (GDR) 4:36.29
1984	Tracy Caulkins (USA) 4:39.24
1988	

4 × 100 Metres Freestyle Relay

1912	Great Britain 5:52.8
1920	United States 5:11.6
1924	United States 4:58.8
1928	United States 4:47.6
1932	United States 4:38.0
1936	Netherlands 4:36.0
1948	United States 4:29.2
1952	Hungary 4:24.4
1956	Australia 4:17.1
1960	United States 4:08.9
1964	United States 4:03.8
1968	United States 4:02.5
1972	United States 3:55.19
1976	United States 3:44.82
1980	GDR 3:42.71
1984	United States 3:43.43
1988	

4 × 100 Metres Medley Relay

1960	United States 4:41.1
1964	United States 4:33.9
1968	United States 4:28.3
1972	United States 4:20.75
1976	GDR 4:07.95
1980	GDR 4:06.67
1984	United States 4:08.34
1988	

Springboard Diving

1920	Aileen Riggin (USA) 539.9
1924	Elizabeth Becker (USA) 474.5
1928	Helen Meany (USA) 78.62
1932	Georgia Coleman (USA) 87.52
1936	Marjorie Gestring (USA) 89.27
1948	Victoria Draves (USA) 108.74
1952	Patricia McCormick (USA) 147.30
1956	Patricia McCormick (USA) 142.36
1960	Ingrid Krämer (GER) 155.81
1964	Ingrid Krämer-Engel (GER) 145.00
1968	Sue Gossick (USA) 150.77
1972	Micki King (USA) 450.03
1976	Jennifer Chandler (USA) 506.19
1980	Irina Kalinina (URS) 725.910
1984	Sylvie Bernier (CAN) 530.70
1988	

Highboard Diving

1912	Greta Johansson (SWE) 39.9
1920	Stefani Fryland-Clausen (DEN) 34.6
1924	Caroline Smith (USA) 10.5
1928	Elizabeth Pinkston (USA) 31.6
1932	Dorothy Poynton (USA) 40.26
1936	Dorothy Poynton-Hill (USA) 33.93
1948	Victoria Draves (USA) 68.87
1952	Patricia McCormick (USA) 79.37
1956	Patricia McCormick (USA) 84.85
1960	Ingrid Krämer (GER) 91.28
1964	Lesley Bush (USA) 99.80
1968	Milena Duchková (TCH) 109.59
1972	Ulrika Knape (SWE) 390.00
1976	Elena Vaytsekhovskaya (URS) 406.59
1980	Martina Jäschke (GDR) 596.250
1984	Jihong Zhou (CHN) 435.51
1988	

Synchronized Swimming – Duet

| 1984 | United States 195.584 |
| 1988 | |

Synchronized Swimming – Solo

| 1984 | Tracie Ruiz (USA) 198.467 |
| 1988 | |

TABLE TENNIS

Debuts with sixty-four men and thirty-two women. Table tennis has never been in the Olympics before, not even as a demonstration sport.

Singles

1988

Doubles

1988

TENNIS

When Charlotte Cooper won the ladies singles in 1900, she became the first woman to win an Olympic championship in any sport. Men's tennis had entered the Games in 1896. Tennis for both sexes was dropped from the Games after 1924, returning as a demonstration sport in 1984 – Steffi Graf won the women's singles – and gaining full Olympic status in 1988. But only forty-eight women compared to sixty-eight men are to play at Seoul.

Singles

1900[1]	Charlotte Cooper (GBR)
1906	Esmeé Simiriotou (GRE)
1908	Dorothea Chambers (GBR)
1908	Gwen Eastlake-Smith (GBR)
1912	Marguerite Broquedis (FRA)
1912	Ethel Hannam (GBR)
1920	Suzanne Lenglen (FRA)
1924	Helen Wills (USA)
1988	

[1] Two bronze medals.

Doubles

1920	Great Britain
1924	United States
1988	

VOLLEYBALL

Men's and women's volleyball were introduced into the Games in 1964. The most successful player, Soviet Union's Inna Ryskal, won two gold and two silver medals between 1964 and 1976.

1964	Japan	1976	Japan	1988	
1968	Soviet Union	1980	Soviet Union		
1972	Soviet Union	1984	China		

YACHTING

In 1908, when she and her husband won the 7m class, Frances Clytie Rivett-Carnac of Britain became the first woman to win an event not restricted to women or mixed pairs in any sport. Women have partnered or served on crews ever since, and in 1988 a women's 470 event will be introduced.

470 Class
1988

NOTES

Chapter 1   Elbowing In

1. Judith Swaddling, *The Ancient Olympic Games*, British Museum, London, 1984, p. 43.
2. *ibid.*, pp. 78–79.
3. *Greek Anthology*, XIII 16, after Drees, in Swaddling, op. cit., p. 42. See L. Drees, *Olympia*, Pall Mall, London, 1968.
4. Philippe Chatrier, *World Tennis*, July 1986, p. 72.
5. 1984/5. Harold Abrahams, *The Olympic Games Book*, James Barrie, London, 1956, p. 29.
6. 'Drugs: A Shock Report', *Athletics Today*, December 1987, pp. 6–16. Most of this is a translation from *Der Spiegel*.

Chapter 2   Dallas Cyclone

1. Most sources give her birth date as 26 June 1914, the date she mentions in her autobiography. She may have been two or three years older. William Oscar Johnson and Nancy P. Williamson, in *'Whatta-Gal': the Babe Didrikson Story*, Little, Brown, Boston, 1977, speak of a late-appearing baptismal certificate which gives her birth as 1911 and cite 1913 as the year she wrote on her application to the 1932 Los Angeles Olympics. Her Olympic fame was based partly on the belief that she was a teenager, something of a prodigy.

    It seems to me, baptismal certificate or no, unlikely that someone as un-academic as Babe, from a family that needed earners, would stay on at school longer than necessary, even with the lure of playing basketball. The baptismal certificate may have been issued well after the fact and be incorrect.
2. This and all other quotations, unless otherwise indicated, come from Johnson and Williamson's book.
3. Charles Landon, *Classic Moments of Athletics*, Ashbourne, Derbyshire, Moorland, 1982, p. 27.
4. N. Gindele's 46.74 metre (153 feet 4 inches) world record throw six weeks earlier was later ratified.
5. Babe Didrikson Zaharias, *Championship Golf*, A. S. Barnes, New York, 1948, p. 14.
6. Dick Patrick, 'No. 1 Female: You judge me' in *USA Today*, September 9, 1987, pp. 9–10.

Chapter 4   Mothers Run Best

1. Fanny Blankers-Koen, 'The Race I Will Never Forget', in Stan Tomlin, ed., *Olympic Odyssey*, Bovril, London, 1956, pp. 44–46. All quotes of Blankers-Koen are from this article.
2. See Michèle Kort, 'Can Maternity Make You a Better Athlete?', *Women's Sports and Fitness*, Palo Alto, California, May 1986, pp. 38–40 & 58; and Alison Turnbull, 'Does Pregnancy Improve Athletic Performance?', *Running Magazine*, London, October 1986, p. 73.

Chapter 5   Deep Water

1. This may be a slight exaggeration. At the height of her fame, she owned 'about two dozen racing costumes – half a dozen in Australian green, some white, some

boldly striped in the colours of Melbourne football teams – and four bikinis'. Dawn Fraser, *Gold Medal Girl: The Confessions of an Olympic Champion*, Nicholas Kaye, London, 1965, p. 14.

2. *ibid.*, p. 7. All other quotes of Fraser are from this book unless otherwise indicated.

Chapter 6   Killer Gymnastics

1. Nadia Comaneci and Graham Buxton Smither, *Nadia, My Own Story*, Proteus, London, 1981, p. 99.
2. See Adrianne Blue, *Grace Under Pressure*, Sidgwick, 1987, pp. 155–166, for a summary of the medical evidence.
3. Alvin Loosli *et al.*, 'Nutrition Habits and Knowledge in Competitive Adolescent Female Gymnasts', *The Physician and Sports Medicine*, August 1986, pp. 118–130.
4. Lionel W. Rosen, *et al.*, 'Pathogenic Weight-Control Behaviour in Female Athletes', *The Physician and Sports Medicine*, January 1986, pp. 79–86.
5. Comaneci, *ibid.*, p. 57.

Chapter 7   Horse Sense

1. Nicholas Courtney, *Princess Anne*, Futura, London, 1987. All quotes of Princess Anne are from this book unless otherwise indicated.
2. Ann Martin, *The Equestrian Woman*, Paddington, New York and London, 1979, p. 87.
3. Caroline Silver, *Eventing*, Collins, London, 1976, p. 150.
4. *ibid.*, p. 146.
5. Martin, *ibid.*, p. 96.
6. Virginia Holgate with Genevieve Murphy, *Ginny*, Stanley Paul, London, 1986, p. 121.

Chapter 8   Soar Like an Eagle, Soar, Soar

1. When she went back with a BBC TV crew in 1978, Tessa Sanderson found the lush physical and emotional warmth she had remembered, but was surprised that the St Elizabeth in which she grew up was also 'very nearly a shanty town'.
2. Tessa Sanderson, *Tessa: My Life in Athletics*, Willow, London, 1986, p. 83. All quotes of Sanderson are from this book.

Chapter 9   Collision Course

1. Neil Macfarlane, *Sport and Politics*, Willow, London, 1986, p. 156.
2. Zola Budd, *Daily Mail*, 13 August, 1984.

Chapter 10   The Perfect Couple

1. John Hennessy, *Torvill & Dean*, David & Charles, London, 1984, p. 13.
2. Christopher Brasher, *Tokyo 1964*, Stanley Paul, London, 1964, p. 78–79.

Chapter 11   The Furthest Race

1. Joan Benoit with Sally Baker, *Running Tide*, Knopf, New York, 1987, p. 165. Most quotes of Benoit are from this book.
2. Joe Falls, *The Boston Marathon*, Collier Macmillan, New York, 1979, p. 93.
3. Jay J. Coakley, *Sport in Society: Issues and Controversies*, St Louis, Times Mirror/Mosby College, 1986.

SELECTED BIBLIOGRAPHY

Benoit, Joan with Sally Baker, *Running Tide*, Knopf, New York, 1987

Blankers-Koen, Fanny, 'The Race I Will Never Forget', in *Olympic Odyssey*, Stan Tomlin, ed., Bovril, London, 1956, pp. 44–46

Blue, Adrianne, *Grace Under Pressure: The Emergence of Women in Sport*, Sidgwick & Jackson, London, 1987

Boutilier, Mary A. and Lucinda SanGiovanni, *The Sporting Woman*, Human Kinetics, Champaign, Illinois, 1983

Brasher, Christopher, *Tokyo 1964*, Stanley Paul, London, 1964

— —, *Mexico 1968*, Stanley Paul, London, 1968

Coakley, Jay J., *Sport in Society: Issues and Controversies*, St Louis, Times Mirror/ Mosby College, 1986

Comaneci, Nadia and Graham Buxton Smither, *Nadia, My Own Story*, Proteus, London, 1981

Coot, James *et al.*, *The Olympics*, ITV Books, London, 1980

Courtney, Nicholas, *Princess Anne*, Futura, London, 1987

Donohoe, Tom and Neil Johnson, *Foul Play: Drug Abuse in Sports*, London, Blackwell, 1986

Drinkwater, Barbara, ed., *Female Endurance Athletes*, Human Kinetics, Champaign, Illinois, 1986

'Drugs: A Shock Report', *Athletics Today*, December 1987, pp. 6–16

Dyer, K. F., *Catching Up the Men: Women in Sport*, Junction, London, 1982

Emery, David and Stan Greenberg, *World Sporting Records*, Bodley Head, London, 1986

Falls, Joe, *The Boston Marathon*, Collier Macmillan, New York, 1979

Fraser, Dawn, *Gold Medal Girl: The Confessions of an Olympic Champion*, Nicholas Kaye, London, 1965

Golubev, Vladimir, *Soviet Gymnastics Stars*, Progress, Moscow, 1979

Graydon, Jan, 'But It's More than a Game', *Feminist Review*, vol. 13, Spring 1983, pp. 5–16

Green, Tina Sloan *et al.*, eds, *Black Women in Sport*, American Alliance for Health, Physical Education, Recreation and Dance, Reston, Virginia, 1981

Greenberg, Stan, *Olympic Games: The Records*, Guinness, Enfield, 1987

Hart-Davis, Duff, *Hitler's Games*, Century, London, 1986

Hemery, David, *Sporting Excellence*, Willow, London, 1986

Hennessy, John, *Torvill & Dean*, David & Charles, London, 1984

Holgate, Virginia with Genevieve Murphy, *Ginny*, Stanley Paul, London, 1986

James, Paul, *Anne: The Working Princess*, Piatkus, London, 1987

Johnson, William Oscar and Nancy P. Williamson, *'Whatta-Gal': The Babe Didrikson Story*, Little, Brown, Boston, 1977

Killanin, Lord and John Rodda, eds, *The Olympic Games*, Willow, London, 1983

Kort, Michèle, 'Can Maternity Make You a Better Athlete?', *Women's Sports and Fitness*, Palo Alto, California, May 1986, pp. 38–40 & 58

Landon, Charles, *Classic Moments of Athletics*, Moorland, Ashbourne, Derby, 1982

Macfarlane, Neil, *Sport and Politics*, Willow, London, 1986

McWhirter, Ross, *The Olympics 1896–1972*, ESSO, London, 1972

Mandell, Richard D., *The Nazi Olympics*, Souvenir, London, 1972

Markel, Robert and Nancy Brooks, *For the Record*, World Almanac, New York, 1985

Martin, Ann, *The Equestrian Woman*, Paddington, New York & London, 1979

Matthews, Peter and Ian Morrison, eds, *The Guinness Encyclopedia of Sports Records & Results*, Guinness, London, 1987

Pannick, David, *Sex Discrimination in Sport*, Equal Opportunities Commission, Manchester, 1983

Regulations for the Olympic Tennis Event, International Tennis Federation, London, 1987

Rhys, Chris, *The Courage Book of Sporting Heroes*, Stanley Paul, London, 1984

Sanderson, Tessa, *Tessa: My Life in Athletics*, Willow, London, 1986

Sport in the GDR: Past and Present, Panorama DDR, 1984

Silver, Caroline, *Eventing*, Collins, London, 1976

'Steroid Abuse', *USA Today*, 6 January 1987

Suleiman, Susan Rubin, ed., *The Female Body in Western Culture*, Harvard, Cambridge, Massachusetts, 1986

Swaddling, Judith, *The Ancient Olympic Games*, British Museum, London, 1984

Tomlinson, Alan and Gerry Whannel, *Five Ring Circus*, Pluto, London, 1984

Tracy, Jim, *Great Sporting Achievements*, Savvas, Adelaide, 1984

Twin, Stephanie, *Out of the Bleachers: Writings on Women and Sport*, Feminist Press, Old Westbury, New York, 1979

Turnbull, Alison, 'Does Pregnancy Improve Athletic Performance?', *Running Magazine*, London, October 1986, p. 73

Wade, Virginia with Jean Rafferty, *Ladies of the Court*, Pavillion, London, 1984

Wells, Christine, *Women, Sport, and Performance: A Physiological Perspective*, Human Kinetics, Champaign, Illinois, 1986

ACKNOWLEDGEMENTS

I am grateful for the invaluable help of Lucinda Montefiore, my editor at Virago.

The photographs are reproduced by kind permission of the following: All-Sport, pp. 13, 21 bottom; 28, 35, 38, 57, 58, 69, 75, 86, 102, 111, 122, 134, 151; Associated Sports Photography, pp. 36, 83, 107, 126, 145; BBC Hulton Picture Library, pp. 5, 7, 46; Culver Pictures, p. 62; Mary Evans Picture Library, pp. 20, 21 top, 29, 40, 41; Popperfoto, p. 97; Chris Smith, pp. x, 16, 63, 78, 87, 100, 106, 132, 136, 141; S & G Press Agency Ltd., p. 121.

INDEX

Page numbers in *italic* refer to the illustrations